also by america's test kitchen

FOR A FULL LISTING OF ALL OUR BOOKS
CooksIllustrated.com
AmericasTestKitchen.com

praise for america's test kitchen titles

"Here are the words just about any vegan would be happy to read: 'Why This Recipe Works.' Fans of America's Test Kitchen are used to seeing the phrase, and now it applies to the growing collection of plant-based creations in *Vegan for Everybody*."

THE WASHINGTON POST ON *VEGAN FOR EVERYBODY*

"True to its name, this smart and endlessly enlightening cookbook is about as definitive as it's possible to get in the modern vegetarian realm."

MEN'S JOURNAL ON *THE COMPLETE VEGETARIAN COOKBOOK*

"This is a wonderful, useful guide to healthy eating."

PUBLISHERS WEEKLY ON *NUTRITIOUS DELICIOUS*

"Another flawless entry in the America's Test Kitchen canon, *Bowls* guides readers of all culinary skill levels in composing one-bowl meals from a variety of cuisines."

BUZZFEED BOOKS ON *BOWLS*

Selected as the Cookbook Award Winner of 2019 in the Health and Special Diet Category

INTERNATIONAL ASSOCIATION OF CULINARY PROFESSIONALS (IACP) ON *THE COMPLETE DIABETES COOKBOOK*

"Diabetics and all health-conscious home cooks will find great information on almost every page."

BOOKLIST (STARRED REVIEW) ON *THE COMPLETE DIABETES COOKBOOK*

"*The Perfect Cookie* . . . is, in a word, perfect. This is an important and substantial cookbook. . . . If you love cookies, but have been a tad shy to bake on your own, all your fears will be dissipated. This is one book you can use for years with magnificently happy results."

THE HUFFINGTON POST ON *THE PERFECT COOKIE*

"The sum total of exhaustive experimentation . . . anyone interested in gluten-free cookery simply shouldn't be without it."

NIGELLA LAWSON ON *THE HOW CAN IT BE GLUTEN-FREE COOKBOOK*

"The book's depth, breadth, and practicality makes it a must-have for seafood lovers."

PUBLISHERS WEEKLY (STARRED REVIEW) ON *FOOLPROOF FISH*

"Offers a real option for a cook who just wants to learn some new ways to encourage family and friends to explore today's sometimes-daunting vegetable universe. This is one of the most valuable vegetable cooking resources for the home chef since Marian Morash's beloved classic *The Victory Garden Cookbook* (1982)."

BOOKLIST (STARRED REVIEW) ON *VEGETABLES ILLUSTRATED*

"If you're a home cook who loves long introductions that tell you why a dish works followed by lots of step-by-step hand holding, then you'll love *Vegetables Illustrated*."

THE WALL STREET JOURNAL ON *VEGETABLES ILLUSTRATED*

" A one-volume kitchen seminar, addressing in one smart chapter after another the sometimes surprising whys behind a cook's best practices. . . . You get the myth, the theory, the science, and the proof, all rigorously interrogated as only America's Test Kitchen can do."

NPR ON *THE SCIENCE OF GOOD COOKING*

"The 21st-century *Fannie Farmer Cookbook* or *The Joy of Cooking*. If you had to have one cookbook and that's all you could have, this one would do it."

CBS SAN FRANCISCO ON *THE NEW FAMILY COOKBOOK*

"The go-to gift book for newlyweds, small families, or empty nesters."

ORLANDO SENTINEL ON *THE COMPLETE COOKING FOR TWO COOKBOOK*

"Some books impress by the sheer audacity of their ambition. Backed by the magazine's famed mission to test every recipe relentlessly until it is the best it can be, this nearly 900-page volume lands with an authoritative wallop."

CHICAGO TRIBUNE ON *THE COOK'S ILLUSTRATED COOKBOOK*

"It might become your 'cooking school,' the only book you'll need to make you a proficient cook, recipes included. . . . You can master the 100 techniques with the easy-to-understand instructions, then apply the skill with the recipes that follow."

THE LITCHFIELD COUNTY TIMES ON *100 TECHNIQUES*

cooking with plant based meat

COOKING WITH

75 vegan and vegetarian recipes
for all your meaty cravings

AMERICA'S TEST KITCHEN

Library of Congress Cataloging-in-Publication Data

Names: America's Test Kitchen (Firm)
Title: Cooking with plant-based meat : 75 vegan and
    vegetarian recipes for all your meaty cravings / America's
    Test Kitchen.
Description: Boston, MA : America's Test Kitchen, [2022] |
    Includes index. | Summary: "A full PDF of book has been
    provided"-- Provided by publisher.
Identifiers: LCCN 2021050946 (print) | LCCN 2021050947
    (ebook) | ISBN 9781954210028 (hardcover) |
    ISBN 9781954210035 (ebook)
Subjects: LCSH: Vegan cooking. | Vegetarian cooking. |
    Meat substitutes. | LCGFT: Cookbooks.
Classification: LCC TX838 .C66 2022 (print) | LCC TX838
    (ebook) | DDC 641.5/6362--dc23/eng/20211028
LC record available at https://lccn.loc.gov/2021050946
LC ebook record available at https://lccn.loc.
    gov/2021050947

AMERICA'S TEST KITCHEN
21 Drydock Avenue, Boston, MA 02210

Printed in Canada
10 9 8 7 6 5 4 3 2 1

Distributed by Penguin Random House Publisher Services
Tel: 800.733.3000

Pictured on front cover **Classic Burgers Your Way (page 40); Weeknight Meaty Chili (page 133); Chorizo and Potato Tacos with Salsa Verde (page 75); Farro Bowl with Butternut Squash, Sausage, and Radicchio (page 123)**

Pictured on back cover **Larb Lettuce Wraps with Lime, Mint, and Cilantro (page 54); Meat-Lover's Veggie Banh Mi (page 61); Sheet-Pan Barbecue Pizza (page 170)**

Editorial Director, Books **Adam Kowit**

Executive Food Editor **Dan Zuccarello**

Deputy Food Editor **Stephanie Pixley**

Senior Editors **Valerie Cimino, Joseph Gitter, Nicole Konstantinakos, and Sara Mayer**

Test Cooks **Samantha Block and Carmen Dongo**

Additional Recipe Development **Carolynn MacKay**

Executive Managing Editor **Debra Hudak**

Book Editor **Sara Zatopek**

Assistant Editor **Emily Rahravan**

Additional Editorial Support **Rachel Schowalter**

Design Director **Lindsey Timko Chandler**

Associate Art Director **Ashley Tenn**

Photography Director **Julie Bozzo Cote**

Photography Producer **Meredith Mulcahy**

Senior Staff Photographers **Steve Klise and Daniel J. van Ackere**

Staff Photographer **Kevin White**

Additional Photography **Carl Tremblay and Joseph Keller**

Food Styling **Catrine Kelty, Chantal Lambeth, Gina McCreadie, Ashley Moore, Elle Simone Scott, Kendra Smith, Daniel J. van Ackere, and Kevin White**

PHOTOSHOOT KITCHEN TEAM

Photo Team and Special Events Manager **Allison Berkey**

Lead Test Cook **Eric Haessler**

Test Cooks **Hannah Fenton, Jacqueline Gochenouer, and Gina McCreadie**

Assistant Test Cooks **Hisham Hassan and Christa West**

Illustration **Ashley Tenn**

Senior Manager, Publishing Operations **Taylor Argenzio**

Imaging Manager **Lauren Robbins**

Production and Imaging Specialists **Tricia Neumyer, Dennis Noble, and Amanda Yong**

Copy Editor **Cheryl Redmond**

Proofreader **Vicki Rowland**

Indexer **Elizabeth Parson**

Chief Creative Officer **Jack Bishop**

Executive Editorial Directors **Julia Collin Davison and Bridget Lancaster**

contents

welcome to america's test kitchen

This book has been tested, written, and edited by the folks at America's Test Kitchen, where curious cooks become confident cooks. Located in Boston's Seaport District in the historic Innovation and Design Building, it features 15,000 square feet of kitchen space including multiple photography and video studios. It is the home of *Cook's Illustrated* magazine and *Cook's Country* magazine and is the workday destination for more than 60 test cooks, editors, and cookware specialists. Our mission is to empower and inspire confidence, community, and creativity in the kitchen.

We start the process of testing a recipe with a complete lack of preconceptions, which means that we accept no claim, no technique, and no recipe at face value. We simply assemble as many variations as possible, test a half-dozen of the most promising, and taste the results blind. We then construct our own recipe and continue to test it, varying ingredients, techniques, and cooking times until we reach a consensus. As we like to say in the test kitchen, "We make the mistakes so you don't have to." The result, we hope, is the best version of a particular recipe, but we realize that only you can be the final judge of our success (or failure). We use the same rigorous approach when we test equipment and taste ingredients.

All of this would not be possible without a belief that good cooking, much like good music, is based on a foundation of objective technique. Some people like spicy foods and others don't, but there is a right way to sauté, there is a best way to cook a pot roast, and there are measurable scientific principles involved in producing perfectly beaten, stable egg whites. Our ultimate goal is to investigate the fundamental principles of cooking to give you the techniques, tools, and ingredients you need to become a better cook. It is as simple as that.

To see what goes on behind the scenes at America's Test Kitchen, check out our social media channels for kitchen snapshots, exclusive content, video tips, and much more. You can watch us work (in our actual test kitchen) by tuning in to *America's Test Kitchen* or *Cook's Country* on public television or on our websites. Listen to *Proof, Mystery Recipe*, and *The Walk-In* (AmericasTestKitchen.com/podcasts) to hear engaging, complex stories about people and food. Want to hone your cooking skills or finally learn how to bake—with an America's Test Kitchen test cook? Enroll in one of our online cooking classes. And you can engage the next generation of home cooks with kid-tested recipes from America's Test Kitchen Kids.

Our community of home recipe testers provides valuable feedback on recipes under development by ensuring that they are foolproof. You can help us investigate the how and why behind successful recipes from your home kitchen. (Sign up at AmericasTestKitchen.com/recipe_testing.)

However you choose to visit us, we welcome you into our kitchen, where you can stand by our side as we test our way to the best recipes in America.

facebook.com/AmericasTestKitchen
instagram.com/TestKitchen
youtube.com/AmericasTestKitchen
tiktok.com/@TestKitchen
twitter.com/TestKitchen
pinterest.com/TestKitchen

AmericasTestKitchen.com
CooksIllustrated.com
CooksCountry.com
OnlineCookingSchool.com
AmericasTestKitchen.com/kids

a plant-based meat primer

the meat of the matter

While meat alternatives are nothing new, really, truly meaty meat alternatives have emerged on the market in only the last few years. Today's meat alternatives are more like the "real thing" than ever, expertly mimicking the taste, texture, and cooking properties of animal meat. At America's Test Kitchen, we know that sinking your teeth into a juicy, perfectly cooked burger can be an almost transcendent experience. We also know there are many reasons for wanting to reduce your animal meat consumption or eliminate it altogether. But whatever your reason for choosing a meatless meal, thanks to plant-based meat you can now enjoy burger bliss—and all your other meaty favorites—any time you like.

You won't find chewy seitan or old-school textured vegetable protein here. Nor will you find instructions for imbuing tofu or tempeh with a semblance of meatiness. Instead, say hello to crispy-crusted burgers and pasta sauce loaded with tender, savory plant-based morsels. Looking for one-pan dinners ready in an hour or less? We've got you covered with recipes like Skillet Bratwurst with Apples and Brussels Sprouts (page 161) and Not-from-a-Box Weeknight Tacos (page 71). You'll also find enchanting internationally inspired dishes, including Lion's Head Meatballs with Cabbage and Rice Noodles (page 107), Keema (page 141), and Mapo Tofu (page 138), and even an array of apps and snacks for sharing.

A quick note about terminology: Some brands call their products "meat," some "burger," and the internet abounds with references to "veggie beef," "meaty grounds," and more. For clarity, throughout this book we refer to realistic meat alternatives as "plant-based meat," or sometimes just "meat" for short—but rest assured that it's always the plant-based variety we're talking about.

But forget about terminology. All you really need to know is this: This book is your ticket to flavor-packed plant-based recipes that will leave everyone at the table sated and satisfied.

know your options

The explosion of innovation in the plant-based meat field means that it's now common to find a huge variety of realistic meat alternatives at your local supermarket. It's these cutting-edge products by companies including Impossible Foods and Beyond Meat that inspired the recipes in this book. Here's our breakdown of the meatiest meat mimickers currently available.

WHAT WE USE

raw bulk meat

Raw bulk plant-based meat is formulated to mimic the qualities of raw ground animal meat. Impossible Burger and Beyond Meat are two of the most recognizable products in this category. Usually sold in refrigerated or frozen packages, the meat is sticky and cohesive, so it's an excellent choice for shaping into burger patties and meatballs—applications where the meat needs to hold a certain shape. You can mix any seasonings or extra ingredients you like right in and shape it however you like. It also works great when crumbled into smaller pieces for taco fillings, meat sauces, and more. Because bulk meat is such a versatile ingredient, it's what we turn to most often; in fact, we developed the recipes throughout this book using both Impossible Foods' and Beyond Meat's bulk products. (For more information about specific bulk meat products, see page 4.)

preformed and seasoned sausages

Like animal-meat sausages, plant-based sausages come in a variety of styles, and some brands even include a plant-based casing to mimic the snap of animal-meat sausage. In recipes that call for crumbled sausage bits, like Spaghetti with Sausage and Spring Vegetables (page 88), we like to mix one of our homemade sausage seasoning blends (pages 10–11) into raw bulk meat. But when whole sausages are called for, as in Bratwurst Sandwiches with Red Potato and Kale Salad (page 65), we prefer the chewy-snappy texture of store-bought.

Read the packaging carefully to make sure you pick up the right style, and know that plant-based sausages vary widely from brand to brand, so you may need to experiment to find your favorite.

CONVENIENT ALTERNATIVES

preformed patties and meatballs

We generally prefer to use raw bulk meat to form our own burger patties and meatballs so that we can incorporate additional seasonings directly into the meat mixture, but preformed store-bought patties and meatballs can be a convenient shortcut. Several of the companies that make bulk plant-based meat also sell preformed products. But there's a price for convenience: It's often more expensive per ounce.

USE WITH CAUTION

meat crumbles

Meat crumbles, sometimes called soy crumbles, are made of pre-cooked and crumbled vegetable protein. We do not recommend using crumbles in applications where the meat needs to be able to hold a certain shape, such as meatballs or patties. Unlike raw bulk meat, crumbles aren't cohesive and will fall apart or be impossible to shape at all. However, crumbles are fine in dishes such as taco fillings and meat sauces where the meat is broken into small, distinct pieces. If you choose to use crumbles in these cases, just substitute an equal amount by weight of crumbles for the bulk meat.

the anatomy of plant-based meat

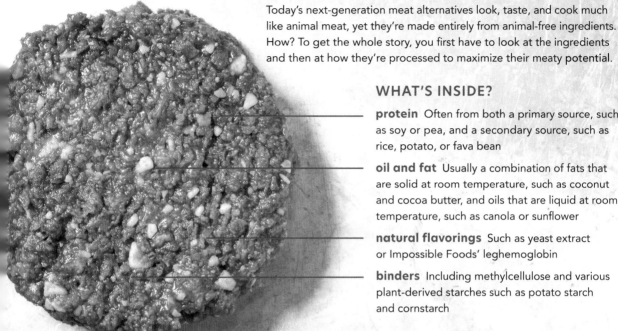

Today's next-generation meat alternatives look, taste, and cook much like animal meat, yet they're made entirely from animal-free ingredients. How? To get the whole story, you first have to look at the ingredients and then at how they're processed to maximize their meaty potential.

WHAT'S INSIDE?

protein Often from both a primary source, such as soy or pea, and a secondary source, such as rice, potato, or fava bean

oil and fat Usually a combination of fats that are solid at room temperature, such as coconut and cocoa butter, and oils that are liquid at room temperature, such as canola or sunflower

natural flavorings Such as yeast extract or Impossible Foods' leghemoglobin

binders Including methylcellulose and various plant-derived starches such as potato starch and cornstarch

HOW DOES IT WORK?

Protein is the main component of plant-based meat. Most products use either pea protein (extracted from dried yellow peas) or soy as their primary protein source, plus a secondary protein to round out the amino acid profile. The proteins are dried, defatted, and ground before being rehydrated and extruded through a machine under heat and pressure to rearrange their structure so they look and feel more like animal meat. Small differences in this process, from the amount of liquid used to how quickly the protein cools off, can have a huge impact on the meat's final texture and appearance.

The **oil and fat** in plant-based meat adds richness and helps distribute aromas and flavors throughout the meat during cooking. The inclusion of saturated fats (fats that are solid at room temperature) like coconut oil and cocoa butter helps keep the meat firmer and easier to work with when chilled. The solid fat also gives the meat a marbled appearance.

Impossible Foods' legume-derived heme protein may be the most talked-about of the **natural flavorings** added to plant-based meat. (Heme is a type of iron-containing molecule.) Like the naturally occurring heme protein in animal meat, Impossible's soy leghemoglobin influences the Maillard reaction to yield the complex savory flavors we associate with browned meat. Other plant-based meat producers use any of a number of yeast extracts to enhance umami flavor and add specific meaty notes. (Fun fact: Yeast extract is the main component of the savory spreads Vegemite and Marmite.)

And because plant-based meat lacks myosin, the sticky protein that helps animal meat hold its shape, it typically includes one or more **binders**. Methylcellulose, derived from the cellulose found in plants' cell walls, is widely used because it's soft at cool temperatures but gels and firms up when heated, so it helps the meat hold on to moisture and achieve that ideal firm-but-yielding bite when cooked.

but how does it taste?

More and more companies are jumping into the plant-based meat arena. To find the best bulk ground products to use to develop our recipes, we rounded up four of the top-selling plant-based meats and tasted them both plain and in burgers topped with lettuce and ketchup. Right away, some clear differences emerged. Our favorite tasted neutrally meaty, whereas others had off flavors or distracting added seasonings. Additionally, some products broke into crumbles readily, while others resisted our efforts. The flavor differences remained apparent even when we conducted a follow-up tasting of the products in a highly seasoned taco filling. Ultimately, however, we found all the products to be acceptable. Nutrition information given is per 3-ounce serving.

highly recommended | comments

Impossible Foods
Impossible Burger

FAT 10.5 g
SUGAR <1 g
SODIUM 278 mg
PROTEIN 14 g

Tasters loved the flavor, texture, and appearance of this product. Of all the products we tasted, this one behaved most like ground beef, picking up good browning and losing its red color when cooked. Its flavor was "mineral-y" and savory, without off flavors or extra seasonings to distract from its meatiness. As one taster summed it up: "If I didn't know that this was made from plants, I would think it was meat."

recommended | comments

Beyond Meat
Beyond Beef

FAT 10.5 g
SUGAR 0 g
SODIUM 225 mg
PROTEIN 15 g

Our tasters very much enjoyed this product. Burgers made with it crisped up nicely and were "juicy" and "firm." It had a "nutty flavor," though some tasters took off points for "strange," "metallic" notes. When eaten plain, it was "salty" and "rich." The cooked meat has a slightly purplish hue, likely due to the beet powder among its ingredients.

recommended with reservations | comments

Morning Star Farms
Incogmeato Plant-Based Ground

FAT 12 g
SUGAR <1 g
SODIUM 300 mg
PROTEIN 15 g

Tasters were pleased with this product's ability to develop a "char on the outside" of the burgers. The burgers "held together well," though some found their interiors a bit too "uniform," "pasty," and "spongy." We had a hard time trying to crumble this product up into small, uniform pieces, ending up with larger, irregular bits instead. And although its flavor was meaty and "inoffensive," some tasters noticed an "artificial" aftertaste.

Pure Farmland
Simply Seasoned Protein Starters

FAT 11 g
SUGAR 0 g
SODIUM 324 mg
PROTEIN 12.5 g

Burgers made with this product developed "a nice crusty exterior." The burgers were juicy and held together well, but some tasters found them "mushy." As its name suggests, this product was well seasoned; many tasters thought the seasoning was "too strong," with clear notes of pepper, onion, and garlic. This product's "very red" color, which didn't fade with cooking, reminded tasters more of chorizo than of beef and made it hard to know when the burgers were done.

and how does it compare?

Cooking with plant-based meat isn't quite as simple as substituting it 1:1 for the animal protein in your favorite meaty recipes. There are a few key differences that are helpful to keep in mind if you're used to cooking with animal meat. Here's the lowdown on what to expect.

start checking for doneness early

it cooks quickly

Plant-based meat cooks faster than animal meat; thick plant-based burger patties, for example, take just 2 to 3 minutes per side compared with 3 to 5 minutes per side for similarly thick beef patties. So pay close attention to recipe cooking times and begin checking for doneness on the early end of the time range to guard against overcooking.

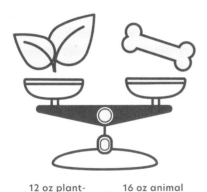

12 oz plant-based meat = 16 oz animal meat

less is more

When exposed to heat, the proteins in plant-based meat don't tighten and shrink as much as animal proteins do. That means plant-based meat loses significantly less volume when cooked compared with beef or pork, so you can use less of it without sacrificing portion size: 12 ounces of cooked plant-based meat is roughly equivalent to 1 pound of cooked animal meat. It also means there's no need to make an indentation in plant-based burger patties before cooking them (a strategy we use to keep beef burgers from doming in the middle as their proteins tighten up).

medium-rare   medium   well-done

it has its own doneness range

Plant-based meat cooked to medium-rare (125 degrees) is mushy and pasty, especially in applications like burgers and meatballs where there's a larger ratio of soft interior to firmer exterior. On the flip side, cooking plant-based meat until well done (160 degrees) yields meat with an unpleasantly bouncy, chewy texture. Most of the cooking time ranges in our recipes are calculated to cook the meat to medium doneness (130 to 135 degrees), which we've found to be the sweet spot for tender, juicy meat.

12 tips for cooking with plant-based meat

SHOP SMART

Different brands have different standard package sizes, so you may need slightly more or less than one package of plant-based meat for our recipes. Check the package carefully to find out how many ounces it contains.

KEEP YOUR HANDS CLEAN

Plant-based meat is pretty sticky, so you'll find your hands coated with the stuff if you don't take proper precautions. Wear food-handling gloves or moisten your hands with water as needed to prevent sticking.

THAW FROZEN MEAT AS NEEDED

Raw bulk plant-based meat keeps longest if stored in the freezer until just before you're ready to use it. If you plan ahead, you can move a package to the fridge to thaw the day before you need it. Or use our quick-thaw method: Seal the frozen meat in a zipper-lock bag (or leave it in its original sealed, watertight packaging) and submerge it in very hot (140-degree) water for 15 to 20 minutes.

HANDLE WITH CARE

Lacking the myosin proteins that help bind animal meat, plant-based meat is softer and more prone to becoming misshapen, especially at room temperature. We work with chilled meat straight from the refrigerator and, after any shaping, re-chill the meat for 15 minutes to allow it to firm it up again before cooking. Be gentle when handling patties or meatballs, and for beautiful spherical meatballs, turn them frequently as they cook.

USE A NONSTICK SKILLET

Plant-based meat doesn't just cling to hands; it can also stick to cooking surfaces, causing patties and meatballs to break apart when you attempt to move them. Avoid this sad state of affairs by using a nonstick skillet as your default pan. (There are a few exceptions to this rule; Shepherd's Pie [page 157], for example, uses a traditional skillet to develop more fond.)

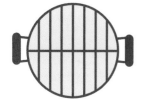

GREASE YOUR GRILL

Likewise, plant-based meat can easily stick to the grill or break apart when flipped, so clean your grill's cooking grate thoroughly and oil it well to prevent sticking.

BECOME FOND OF FOND

The Maillard reaction is the process, signaled by browning, by which heat causes proteins and sugars in foods to change their chemical makeup and form hundreds of new flavor compounds. Take advantage of this process and deepen the flavor of your plant-based meals by cooking plant-based meat until it develops a dark, crispy crust, and then scrape up the fond (the browned bits left on the bottom and sides of the pan) with a wooden spoon to incorporate its flavor back into the dish.

KEEP AN EYE ON THE MEAT

Visual cues can help you determine the doneness of plant-based meat just as they do for animal meat, but what you'll need to look for is different. Don't rely on the color of the meat, as this varies by brand. Instead, you'll know that the meat has just reached the doneness sweet spot when it starts separating into firm crumbles, or is well browned and registers 130 to 135 degrees.

REVERSE THE STANDARD COOKING ORDER

In recipes using animal meat, we often call for browning the meat before adding the other ingredients. But because plant-based meat cooks through so quickly, it's better to do the opposite: Start your aromatics and longer-cooking vegetables first, adding the meat only once the aromatics and vegetables are softened.

USE LESS SALT

Salt is added to plant-based meat during processing. While the sodium content varies by product, we've found that we can use ¼ teaspoon less salt overall in recipes made with plant-based meat than in equivalent recipes made with animal meat.

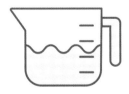

ADD EXTRA LIQUID TO SAUCY DISHES

Although you may see a little moisture or fat left in the pan when cooking plant-based meat, it tends to release a smaller amount of liquid than animal meat does when cooked. We compensate for this by adding extra liquid (usually water or broth), to saucy dishes like chili, taco fillings, and casseroles to achieve the ideal consistency.

REFREEZE LEFTOVERS

If you have a few ounces of thawed meat left over from a package after making a recipe, you can refreeze it with no loss of texture or quality (unlike with animal meat). Just seal the meat in an airtight container and pop it back into the freezer for up to six months. (For more ways to use up leftover meat, see page 11.)

meaty flavor boosters

Plant-based meat manufacturers work hard to make their products taste rich and satisfying, and their carefully calibrated formulas include special umami-enhancing natural flavorings you won't find in any grocery store. (See page 3 for more information about the ingredients plant-based meat companies use to make their products taste meatier.) But you don't have to be a food scientist to cook up flavorful meatless meals. There are plenty of readily available plant-based foods that are rich in the naturally occurring amino acids and nucleotides that make them taste complex and deeply savory—meaty, even. Other ingredients may not taste meaty on their own but are a vital part of the equation when seeking to imitate the flavor profiles of seasoned meats like sausage or chorizo. Here are the ingredients we turn to time and time again to take plant-based meat to the next level.

soy sauce/tamari

Soy sauce is made from fermented soybeans, salt, water, and sometimes roasted grains (wheat, rice, or barley). Tamari is a Japanese form of soy sauce that is generally gluten-free (read the label carefully to be sure). We add extra soy sauce to our Bun Cha (page 108) to give it the salty seasoning and slightly funky savoriness that's provided by fish sauce in traditional versions.

miso

Miso paste is a fermented condiment made from soybeans, grains like rice or barley, salt, and koji mold. It comes in a range of colors, from milder, sweeter white miso to more intense red and brown misos. The miso sauce in our Savory Soba Noodles with Eggplant and Miso (page 104) is salty, nutty, and rich in umami.

tomatoes and tomato products

Tomatoes, especially their seeds and pulp, are packed with flavor-enhancing glutamates that contribute to umami. Sun-dried tomatoes and canned tomato products, particularly tomato paste, contain less moisture and thus have a more concentrated umami flavor, giving depth to dishes such as Shepherd's Pie (page 157).

nutritional yeast

Different from the yeast extracts that manufacturers add to plant-based meat (see page 3), nutritional yeast is yeast that has been deactivated with heat to remove its leavening qualities and then dried into a flaky yellow powder. This umami powerhouse brings uniquely nutty, cheesy flavors to foods, including Meaty Loaded Nacho Dip (page 16).

mushrooms

Drying mushrooms concentrates their umami content, so look to pantry-friendly dried mushrooms such as porcini to boost the savory flavor of dishes such as Italian Wedding Soup (page 126). Fresh mushrooms also pack plenty of oomph in dishes like One-Pot Stroganoff (page 100).

olives

No matter how they are cured (with brine, oil, or salt), olives have a decidedly meaty texture, but they also have a salty, savory flavor that makes them a go-to umami enhancer in many meatless dishes, such as Toasted Orzo Pilaf with Meatballs, Fennel, and Orange (page 99).

smoked paprika

Smoked paprika is made from red peppers that are dried over oak embers and then ground. The resulting spice is sweetly savory with a woodsy smokiness. We use it to deliver smoky flavor fast in Grilled Smokehouse Barbecue Burgers (page 42).

fennel seeds

Fennel seeds don't bring meaty qualities per se, but they are essential when re-creating the flavor profile of certain iconic meaty foods, like sausage, using plant-based ingredients. They're a crucial ingredient in our Breakfast Sausage Seasoning (page 10) and Italian sausage seasonings (page 11).

cider vinegar

Mexican chorizo is heavily seasoned, rich, and tangy—the last of which is due to the inclusion of fruity, piquant cider vinegar. For our plant-based version, featured in recipes including Chorizo and Potato Tacos with Salsa Verde (page 75), adding a hefty splash of cider vinegar to the meat mixture is a must.

what is umami? "Umami" translates from Japanese literally as "deliciousness," but this fifth taste sensation of the five basic tastes (along with sweet, sour, bitter, and salty) is aptly described as "savoriness" or "meatiness." The presence of certain amino acids (the building blocks of proteins) and nucleotides (the building blocks of DNA and RNA) in food creates a deep, complex intensity of flavor that leaves you wanting more. Umami is often associated with meats or cheeses, but it was actually first identified in relation to seaweed. Glutamate—the primary amino acid associated with umami flavor—and other umami-producing nucleotides such as inosinate and guanylate are common and naturally occurring substances found in many plant-based products. In addition, some food preservation techniques, including fermentation, aging, and drying, can increase the amount of umami impact an ingredient brings to the table.

plant-based basics

We keep these high-powered seasoning blends on hand for making plant-based meatballs, sausage, and chorizo; each blend makes enough for 12 ounces of plant-based meat. For fresh alternatives to store-bought, try our recipes for plant-based mayonnaise, Parmesan, and ricotta. And for pastries both savory and sweet, try our Plant-Based Pie Dough.

italian meatball seasoning

makes about 1 teaspoon
total time 5 minutes

Garlic powder and dried oregano provide plenty of zesty Italian meatball flavor.

- ½ teaspoon garlic powder
- ¼ teaspoon dried oregano
- ¼ teaspoon table salt
- ⅛ teaspoon pepper

Combine all ingredients in small bowl. (Spice blend can be stored in airtight container for up to 1 month.)

breakfast sausage seasoning

makes about 4 teaspoons
total time 5 minutes

Stir this blend into plant-based meat for breakfast sausages that nimbly toe the line between savory, earthy, and sweet.

- 1¼ teaspoons garlic powder
- 1¼ teaspoons packed light brown sugar
- 1 teaspoon dried sage
- ½ teaspoon pepper
- ¼ teaspoon dried thyme
- ⅛ teaspoon table salt
  Pinch cayenne pepper

Combine all ingredients in small bowl. (Spice blend can be stored in airtight container for up to 1 month.)

sweet italian sausage seasoning

makes about 1 tablespoon
total time 5 minutes

The fennel seeds in this blend give plant-based meat an immediately recognizable Italian sausage flavor.

1½	teaspoons fennel seeds, lightly crushed
1	teaspoon dried thyme
¾	teaspoon sugar
¼	teaspoon garlic powder
⅛	teaspoon red pepper flakes

Combine all ingredients in small bowl. (Spice blend can be stored in airtight container for up to 1 month.)

variation

hot italian sausage seasoning
Reduce sugar to ¼ teaspoon and increase red pepper flakes to ½ teaspoon.

mexican chorizo seasoning

makes about 5 tablespoons
total time 5 minutes

This nuanced blend adds herbal, warmly spiced flair to burgers, tacos, and more.

4	teaspoons ancho chile powder
4	teaspoons paprika
2	teaspoons ground cumin
1	teaspoon ground coriander
2	teaspoons dried oregano
2	teaspoons sugar
½	teaspoon garlic powder
½	teaspoon ground cinnamon
	Pinch cayenne pepper
	Pinch ground allspice

Combine all ingredients in small bowl. (Spice blend can be stored in airtight container for up to 1 month.)

got leftovers? Transform leftover meat into easy meatballs or breakfast patties that you can freeze and heat up whenever you like. This method also works equally well with larger amounts of meat.

to make meatballs: Per 4 ounces plant-based meat, combine ¼ teaspoon Italian Meatball Seasoning, 2 tablespoons panko bread crumbs, and 2 teaspoons water with meat. Roll mixture into 1½-inch balls, place on plate, and freeze until solid, then transfer frozen meatballs to zipper-lock bag. When ready to use, thaw meatballs overnight in refrigerator, then sear (in 1 tablespoon oil in 12-inch nonstick skillet over medium-high heat) or simmer until registering at least 130 degrees. Alternatively, roast meatballs from frozen on rimmed baking sheet in 475-degree oven until meatballs are browned on all sides and register at least 130 degrees.

to make breakfast patties: Per 4 ounces plant-based meat, combine 1¼ teaspoons Breakfast Sausage Seasoning with meat. Divide meat mixture into balls, then flatten balls into ½-inch-thick patties, place on plate, and freeze until solid; transfer frozen patties to zipper-lock bag. When ready to use, thaw patties overnight in refrigerator or cook from frozen; cook in 1 tablespoon oil in 12-inch nonstick skillet over medium-high heat until patties are well browned on both sides and register at least 130 degrees.

plant-based mayonnaise

makes about 1 cup
total time 15 minutes

Aquafaba, the liquid in canned chickpeas, gives this egg-free mayo emulsified body. One can of chickpeas will yield at least ⅓ cup aquafaba. If you'd rather use store-bought mayonnaise, we like Just Mayo.

⅓	cup (2⅔ ounces) aquafaba
1½	teaspoons lemon juice
½	teaspoon table salt
½	teaspoon sugar
½	teaspoon Dijon mustard
1¼	cups vegetable oil
3	tablespoons extra-virgin olive oil

1 Process aquafaba, lemon juice, salt, sugar, and mustard in food processor for 10 seconds. With processor running, gradually add vegetable oil in slow steady stream until mixture is thick and creamy, scraping down sides of bowl as needed, about 3 minutes.

2 Transfer mixture to bowl. Whisking constantly, slowly add olive oil until emulsified. If pools of oil form on surface, stop addition of oil and whisk mixture until well combined, then resume adding oil. Mayonnaise should be thick and glossy with no oil pools on surface. (Mayonnaise can be refrigerated for up to 1 week.)

plant-based parmesan

makes about 1 cup
total time 50 minutes

To satisfy our cravings for the savory punch of grated Parmesan, we created this dairy-free substitute with rich nuts, briny olives, and cheesy nutritional yeast. This winning combo even has a texture similar to that of the crystalline bits in high-quality aged Parmesan.

¾ cup raw cashews
3 tablespoons nutritional yeast
2 tablespoons raw pine nuts
1 tablespoon chopped green olives, patted dry
¾ teaspoon table salt

1 Adjust oven rack to middle position and heat oven to 275 degrees. Process all ingredients in food processor until finely ground, about 1 minute, scraping down sides of bowl as needed.

2 Spread mixture on rimmed baking sheet in even layer. Bake until mixture is light golden and dry to touch, about 20 minutes, stirring mixture and rotating pan halfway through baking.

3 Let mixture cool completely, about 15 minutes. Break apart any large clumps before serving. (Parmesan can be refrigerated for up to 1 month.)

cashew ricotta

makes about 1 cup
total time 10 minutes, plus 8 hours soaking

Cashew ricotta is creamy, dreamy, and easy to make at home. Plus, it's easy to customize endlessly with additional seasonings and mix-ins. But do plan ahead: The raw cashews need to soak for at least 8 hours before processing.

1 cup raw cashews
2 tablespoons extra-virgin olive oil
2 teaspoons lemon juice, plus extra for seasoning
¼ teaspoon table salt

1 Place cashews in bowl and add water to cover by 1 inch. Soak cashews at room temperature for at least 8 hours or up to 24 hours. Drain and rinse well.

2 Process cashews, ¼ cup water, oil, lemon juice, and salt in food processor until smooth, about 2 minutes, scraping down sides of bowl as needed. Adjust consistency with additional water as needed. Season with salt, pepper, and extra lemon juice to taste. (Ricotta can be refrigerated for up to 1 week.)

variations
cashew ricotta with roasted red peppers
In step 2, add ½ cup rinsed and chopped roasted red peppers, 1 minced garlic clove, and ½ teaspoon pepper to processor with cashews. After processing, stir in ½ cup minced fresh parsley.

cashew ricotta with chipotle and lime
Add ½ teaspoon chipotle chile powder and ½ teaspoon ground cumin to processor with cashews. Substitute lime juice for lemon juice. After processing, stir in 2 tablespoons minced fresh cilantro.

cashew ricotta with sun-dried tomatoes and rosemary
Add 2 teaspoons minced fresh rosemary to processor with cashews. After processing, stir in ½ cup finely chopped oil-packed sun-dried tomatoes.

plant-based pie dough

makes two 9-inch rounds
total time 15 minutes

This pie dough relies on coconut oil for its flakiness. As with butter, coconut oil becomes harder or softer depending on the ambient temperature, so be sure the coconut oil has the right consistency before beginning: It should be just soft enough to pinch into pieces with your fingers. If the oil is too hard, let it sit in a warm place until soft. If the oil is liquefied, let it sit in the refrigerator until firmer. To avoid ragged edges when rolling out the dough, press firmly on the sides to seal any cracks when forming it into disks and allow the dough to sit at room temperature for a few minutes to soften before rolling.

- 3 cups (15 ounces) all-purpose flour, divided
- 1 tablespoon sugar
- 1 teaspoon table salt
- 1 cup plus 2 tablespoons refined coconut oil
- ½ cup ice water, plus extra as needed

1 Process 1½ cups flour, sugar, and salt in food processor until combined, about 5 seconds. Pinch off ½-inch pieces of oil into flour mixture and pulse until sticky and dough just begins to clump, 12 to 16 pulses. (If mixture has paste-like consistency, chill in refrigerator until firm.) Redistribute dough evenly around processor blade, add remaining 1½ cups flour, and pulse until just incorporated, 3 to 6 pulses; transfer to large bowl.

2 Sprinkle ice water over mixture. Stir and press dough with spatula until dough sticks together, being careful not to overmix. If dough doesn't come together, stir in up to 2 tablespoons ice water, 2 teaspoons at a time, until it does. Using spatula, divide dough into 2 equal portions. Transfer each portion to sheet of plastic wrap and form each into 4-inch disk. (Dough can be wrapped tightly in plastic wrap and refrigerated for up to 2 days or frozen for up to 1 month. Let dough sit at room temperature to soften completely before rolling out, about 2 hours if refrigerated or 4 hours if frozen.)

tips for terrific plant-based dough

if the dough looks pebbly and won't come together . . . the coconut oil may be too cold. Let the dough sit in a warm place for a few minutes before proceeding. If the dough clumps in step 1 but doesn't come together in step 2, add up to 2 tablespoons of ice water in small increments until the dough comes together.

if the dough looks loose . . . cover it loosely with plastic wrap and refrigerate until it firms up.

if the dough is hard to roll out after refrigerating . . . leave it on the counter at room temperature until malleable, anywhere from 2 to 15 minutes depending on the temperature of your kitchen.

too dry

too loose

just right

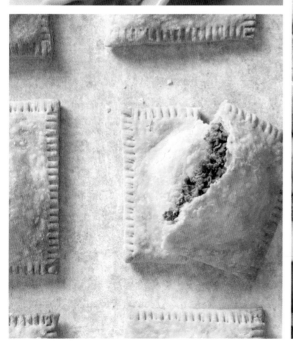

chapter 1
snacks and apps

meaty loaded nacho dip

serves 8

total time 45 minutes

12 ounces russet potatoes, peeled and cut into 1-inch pieces

1 small carrot, peeled and cut into ½-inch pieces (⅓ cup)

3 tablespoons vegetable oil, divided

1½ tablespoons nutritional yeast

1½ teaspoons distilled white vinegar

1⅛ teaspoons table salt, divided

1 teaspoon minced canned chipotle chile in adobo sauce, divided

⅛ teaspoon mustard powder

1 small red onion, chopped fine, divided

⅓ cup minced poblano chile

1 garlic clove, minced

⅛ teaspoon ground cumin

⅛ teaspoon ground coriander

4 ounces plant-based ground meat

2 ounces cherry or grape tomatoes, quartered

2 tablespoons chopped fresh cilantro

why this recipe works Once you've tasted it, you'll see why this gooey, stick-to-your-ribs hot dip is mandatory fare at any Big Game watch party. The subtly spicy meaty topping, made with plant-based meat, poblano chile, onion, and garlic, delivers a powerful flavor punch that makes this dip the MVP of any snack spread. And the award for best team player goes to the plant-based nacho sauce, which gets its amazingly cheese-like consistency from a potato. That's right—a potato. Purposefully overprocessing a cooked russet potato in a blender releases its abundant starch, which gives the dip its thick, cheesy texture. We also blend in carrot for color, chipotle chile for smoky spiciness, nutritional yeast for funky flavor depth, and vegetable oil for fluidity. Scooped up with crunchy tortilla chips, this loaded dip is a winner. We love the dip garnished with chopped red onion, tomatoes, and cilantro, but you can also add chopped avocado, fresh or pickled jalapeños, or sliced scallions. To rewarm cooled dip, microwave it, covered, in 30-second bursts, whisking at each interval and thinning with water as needed, or rewarm it on the stovetop, whisking occasionally and thinning with water as needed.

1 Bring 2 quarts water to boil in medium saucepan over high heat. Add potatoes and carrot and cook until tender, about 12 minutes; drain well. Combine cooked vegetables, ⅓ cup water, 2 tablespoons oil, nutritional yeast, vinegar, 1 teaspoon salt, ½ teaspoon chipotle, and mustard powder in blender. Pulse until chopped and combined, about 10 pulses, scraping down sides of blender jar as needed. (You will need to stop processing to scrape down sides of blender jar several times for mixture to come together.) Process mixture on high speed until very smooth, about 2 minutes. Season with salt and pepper to taste.

2 While vegetables cook, heat remaining 1 tablespoon oil in 10-inch nonstick skillet over medium heat until shimmering. Add two-thirds of onion, poblano, and remaining ⅛ teaspoon salt and cook until softened and lightly browned, 5 to 7 minutes. Stir in garlic, cumin, coriander, and remaining ½ teaspoon chipotle and cook until fragrant, about 30 seconds. Add ground meat and cook, breaking up meat with wooden spoon, until firm crumbles form, about 2 minutes.

3 Transfer dip to serving bowl and top with meat mixture. Sprinkle with tomatoes, cilantro, and remaining onion. Serve.

lemony hummus with baharat-spiced topping

serves 12 to 14
total time 45 minutes

hummus

⅓ cup lemon juice (2 lemons), plus extra for seasoning

3 garlic cloves, minced to paste (1 tablespoon)

1 teaspoon table salt

2 (15-ounce) cans chickpeas, rinsed

¼ cup water, plus extra as needed

½ cup tahini

2 tablespoons extra-virgin olive oil

topping

1 tablespoon extra-virgin olive oil, plus extra for drizzling

¼ cup finely chopped onion

2 garlic cloves, minced

1 teaspoon hot smoked paprika

1 teaspoon ground cumin

¼ teaspoon pepper

¼ teaspoon ground coriander

⅛ teaspoon ground cloves

⅛ teaspoon ground cinnamon

8 ounces plant-based ground meat

⅓ cup pine nuts, toasted, divided

2 teaspoons lemon juice

1 teaspoon chopped fresh parsley

why this recipe works Topping hummus with richly spiced beef is a popular practice throughout the Middle East. Here, warm spices meld with juicy plant-based ground meat and crunchy toasted pine nuts. Such a fantastically flavorful topping deserves an equally flavorful homemade hummus, and this simple version comes together in a snap in a food processor. Topped with the meat mixture and served with pita and crudités, this is no ordinary bean dip. Toast the pine nuts in a dry skillet over medium-high heat until fragrant, 3 to 5 minutes. The hummus will thicken slightly over time; add warm water, 1 tablespoon at a time, as needed to restore its creamy consistency. You can gently warm the hummus in the microwave to make it even smoother.

1 for the hummus: Whisk lemon juice, garlic, and salt together in bowl and let sit for 10 minutes. Strain garlic-lemon mixture through fine-mesh strainer set over second bowl, pressing on solids to extract as much liquid as possible; discard solids.

2 Process chickpeas, water, and garlic-lemon mixture in food processor until smooth, about 1 minute, scraping down sides of bowl as needed. Add tahini and oil and process until hummus is smooth, creamy, and light, about 1 minute, scraping down sides of bowl as needed. (Hummus should have pourable consistency similar to yogurt. If too thick, loosen with water, adding 1 teaspoon at a time.) Season with salt and extra lemon juice to taste. (Hummus can be refrigerated for up to 5 days. Let sit, covered, at room temperature for 30 minutes before serving.)

3 for the topping: Heat oil in 12-inch nonstick skillet over medium heat until shimmering. Add onion and garlic and cook, stirring occasionally, until onion is softened, about 4 minutes. Add paprika, cumin, pepper, coriander, cloves, and cinnamon and cook, stirring constantly, until fragrant, about 30 seconds. Add ground meat and cook, breaking up meat with wooden spoon, until firm crumbles form, 2 to 3 minutes. Stir in ¼ cup pine nuts and lemon juice.

4 Transfer hummus to wide, shallow serving bowl. Using back of spoon, make 1-inch-deep well in center of hummus, leaving 1-inch border. Spoon topping into well in hummus. Sprinkle with parsley and remaining pine nuts and drizzle with extra oil. Serve.

summer rolls

serves 4 to 6 (makes 12 rolls)

total time 55 minutes

peanut-hoisin sauce

- 1 Thai chile, sliced thin
- 1 garlic clove, minced
- 1 teaspoon kosher salt
- ⅔ cup water
- ⅓ cup creamy peanut butter
- 3 tablespoons hoisin sauce
- 2 tablespoons tomato paste
- 1 tablespoon distilled white vinegar

summer rolls

- 6 ounces rice vermicelli
- 1 tablespoon vegetable oil
- 12 ounces plant-based ground meat
- 1 cup fresh mint leaves
- 1 cup fresh cilantro leaves and thin stems
- 1 cup fresh Thai basil leaves
- 12 (8½-inch) round rice paper wrappers
- 12 leaves red or green leaf lettuce, thick ribs removed
- 2 scallions, sliced thin on bias

why this recipe works Loaded with springy rice noodles, crisp lettuce, and an abundance of fresh herbs, Vietnamese summer rolls are a cool delight. Our version replaces the pork and shrimp that traditionally add protein to these rolls with savory plant-based ground meat, which complements the freshness of mint, cilantro, and Thai basil as well as the spicy-sweet dipping sauce. To soften the rice paper wrappers, we dunk them briefly in cold water and then transfer them to the counter while still stiff. This leaves them with just enough moisture clinging to the surface to hydrate and become elastic enough to support a generous amount of filling while remaining easy to handle. For the best results, make sure to shake all excess water from the noodles after rinsing them. A wooden surface will draw moisture away from the wrappers, so assemble the rolls directly on your counter or on a plastic cutting board. If part of the wrapper starts to dry out while you are forming the rolls, moisten it with your dampened fingers. If Thai basil is unavailable, increase the mint and cilantro to 1½ cups each.

1 for the peanut-hoisin sauce: Using mortar and pestle (or on cutting board using flat side of chef's knife), mash Thai chile, garlic, and salt to fine paste. Transfer to medium bowl. Add water, peanut butter, hoisin, tomato paste, and vinegar and whisk until smooth; set aside for serving. (Sauce can be refrigerated for up to 4 days; let come to room temperature before serving.)

2 for the summer rolls: Bring 2 quarts water to boil in medium saucepan. Off heat, add noodles and let sit until tender, about 10 minutes. Drain noodles and rinse with cold water until cool. Drain noodles again, then spread on large plate to dry.

3 Heat oil in 12-inch nonstick skillet over medium heat until shimmering. Add ground meat and cook, breaking up meat with wooden spoon, until firm crumbles form, about 3 minutes. Off heat, let cool completely.

4 Tear mint, cilantro, and Thai basil into 1-inch pieces and combine in bowl. Fill large bowl with cold water. Submerge 1 wrapper in water until wet on both sides, no longer than 2 seconds. Shake gently over bowl to remove excess water, then lay wrapper flat on work surface (wrapper will be fairly stiff but will continue to soften as you assemble roll). Repeat with second wrapper and place next to first wrapper. Fold 1 lettuce leaf and

place on lower third of first wrapper, leaving about ½-inch margin on each side. Spread ⅓ cup noodles on top of lettuce, then sprinkle with 1 teaspoon scallions. Top scallions with 2 heaping tablespoons meat. Spread ¼ cup herb mixture over meat.

5 Bring lower edge of wrapper up and over herbs. Roll snugly but gently until long sides of greens and noodles are enclosed. Fold in sides to enclose ends and continue to roll until filling is completely enclosed in neat cylinder. Transfer roll to serving platter and cover with plastic wrap. Repeat with second moistened wrapper. Repeat with remaining wrappers and filling, keeping completed rolls covered with plastic. Uncover and serve immediately with sauce. (Leftover rolls can be wrapped tightly in plastic and refrigerated for up to 24 hours, but wrappers will become chewier and may break in places.)

egg rolls

serves 4 to 6 (makes 8 rolls)
total time 50 minutes

soy-vinegar dipping sauce

¼ cup soy sauce

2 tablespoons water

4 teaspoons distilled
  white vinegar

2 teaspoons sugar

1 scallion, sliced thin (optional)

egg rolls

1 teaspoon vegetable oil

8 ounces plant-based
  ground meat

6 scallions, white and green
  parts separated and
  sliced thin

3 garlic cloves, minced

2 teaspoons grated fresh
  ginger

3 cups shredded green
  cabbage

4 ounces shiitake mushrooms,
  stemmed and chopped

1 carrot, peeled and shredded

3 tablespoons soy sauce

1 tablespoon sugar

1 tablespoon distilled
  white vinegar

2 teaspoons toasted sesame oil

8 (8-inch) square plant-based or
  egg-based egg roll wrappers

2 cups peanut or vegetable oil
  for frying

why this recipe works These crispy little umami bundles are stuffed with savory plant-based meat sautéed with aromatic ginger and garlic, scallions, cabbage, shiitake mushrooms, and carrots. Here, the plant-based meat acts as a substantial backdrop that allows all the bold flavors of the add-ins to shine. Shallow-frying the rolls in just ½ inch of oil and in a skillet rather than deep-frying them makes the cooking easier and the cleanup faster while still ensuring that the rolls crisp to a beautiful golden brown. All that's left is to whip up a dipping sauce: A salty-tangy-sweet sauce perfectly sets off these umami-packed rolls. This recipe can be easily doubled to feed a crowd: Fry the egg rolls in two batches. Serve the egg rolls with Chinese hot mustard and/or duck sauce, if desired.

1 for the soy-vinegar dipping sauce: Whisk all ingredients (including scallion, if using) in bowl until sugar has dissolved; set aside for serving. (Sauce can be refrigerated for up to 4 days; allow to come to room temperature before serving.)

2 for the egg rolls: Heat vegetable oil in 12-inch nonstick skillet over medium heat until shimmering. Add ground meat and cook, breaking up meat with wooden spoon, until firm crumbles form, 2 to 3 minutes. Add scallion whites, garlic, and ginger and cook until fragrant, about 1 minute. Add cabbage, mushrooms, carrot, soy sauce, sugar, and vinegar and cook until cabbage is just softened, 3 to 5 minutes.

3 Off heat, stir in sesame oil and scallion greens. Transfer meat mixture to large plate, spread into even layer, and refrigerate until cool enough to handle, about 5 minutes. Wipe skillet clean with paper towels.

4 Fill small bowl with water. Working with 1 wrapper at a time, arrange on counter so 1 corner points toward edge of counter. Place ⅓ cup filling on lower half of wrapper and mold it with your fingers into neat 4-inch-long cylinder parallel to edge of counter. Dip your fingertips in water and moisten entire border of wrapper with thin film of water.

5 Fold bottom corner of wrapper up and over filling and press it down on other side of filling. Fold both side corners of wrapper in over filling and press gently to seal. Roll filling up over itself until wrapper is fully sealed. Transfer egg roll seam side down to parchment paper–lined plate and cover with damp paper towel while shaping remaining egg rolls. Stack egg rolls as needed, separating layers with additional parchment. (Egg rolls can be wrapped tightly in plastic wrap and refrigerated for up to 24 hours. Alternatively, freeze egg rolls on plate, then transfer to zipper-lock bag and freeze for up to 1 month. Do not thaw before cooking; increase cooking time by about 1 minute per side.)

6 Set wire rack in rimmed baking sheet and line rack with triple layer of paper towels. Heat peanut oil in now-empty skillet over medium-high heat to 350 degrees. Using tongs, carefully add egg rolls seam side down to hot oil and cook until deep golden brown, 4 to 8 minutes, flipping egg rolls halfway through frying. Adjust burner, if necessary, to maintain oil temperature between 325 and 350 degrees. Using tongs, transfer egg rolls to prepared rack and let drain. Serve with sauce.

stuffed grape leaves

serves 8 to 12
(makes 24 stuffed leaves)

total time 2 hours, plus
30 minutes cooling

1 (16-ounce) jar grape leaves

2 tablespoons extra-virgin
olive oil, plus extra for serving

1 large onion, chopped fine

¼ teaspoon table salt

8 ounces plant-based
ground meat

¾ cup short-grain white rice

1 teaspoon ground cumin

½ teaspoon ground allspice

¼ cup chopped fresh mint

2 teaspoons grated lemon zest
plus 2 tablespoons juice, plus
lemon wedges for serving

why this recipe works Adding plant-based meat to the traditional rice-and-herb filling in Greek dolmathes gives these small bites so much appeal and staying power that they'd be just as appropriate as a light dinner as they would be on a meze platter. We cook the meat just until it's no longer raw and then combine it with parcooked rice, spices, mint, and lemon zest to make a fragrant and cohesive filling that won't spill out of the leaves. About those leaves: Since they're packed in brine, we blanch them briefly in boiling water to wash away excess salt. We also use some of the extras to line the bottom of the skillet to prevent the stuffed leaves from scorching. After gently simmering the stuffed leaves until tender, we like to drizzle them with fruity olive oil for a rich finish. Larger grape leaves can be trimmed to 6 inches, and smaller leaves can be overlapped to achieve the correct size. You can use long-grain rice instead of short-grain rice, but the filling will not be as cohesive.

1 Reserve 24 intact grape leaves, roughly 6 inches in diameter; set aside remaining leaves. Bring 6 cups water to boil in medium saucepan. Add reserved grape leaves and cook for 1 minute. Gently drain leaves and transfer to bowl of cold water to cool, about 5 minutes. Drain again, then transfer leaves to plate and cover loosely with plastic wrap.

2 Heat oil in now-empty saucepan over medium heat until shimmering. Add onion and salt and cook until softened, about 5 minutes. Add ground meat and cook, breaking up meat with wooden spoon, until firm crumbles form, 2 to 3 minutes. Add rice, cumin, and allspice and cook, stirring frequently, until fragrant, about 2 minutes. Stir in ¾ cup water and scrape up any browned bits. Reduce heat to low, cover, and simmer gently until water has been absorbed, about 5 minutes. Off heat, let rice cool slightly, about 10 minutes. Stir in mint and lemon zest.

3 Place 1 blanched leaf smooth side down on counter with stem facing you. Remove stem from base of leaf by cutting along both sides of stem to form narrow triangle. Pat leaf dry with paper towels. Overlap cut ends of leaf to prevent any filling from spilling out. Place heaping tablespoon filling ¼ inch from bottom of leaf where ends overlap. Fold bottom over filling and fold in sides. Roll leaf tightly around filling to create tidy roll. Repeat with remaining blanched leaves and remaining filling.

4 Line 12-inch skillet with single layer of remaining leaves. Place rolled leaves seam side down in tight rows in prepared skillet. Add 1¼ cups water and lemon juice to skillet and bring to simmer over medium heat. Cover, reduce heat to medium-low, and simmer until water is almost completely absorbed and leaves and rice are tender and cooked through, 45 minutes to 1 hour.

5 Transfer stuffed grape leaves to serving platter and let cool completely, about 30 minutes; discard leaves in skillet. (Stuffed grape leaves can be refrigerated for up to 3 days; let come to room temperature before serving.) Drizzle with extra oil and serve with lemon wedges.

classic pub sliders

serves 8
total time 1 hour

burger sauce

- 2 tablespoons plant-based or egg-based mayonnaise
- 1 tablespoon ketchup
- 1 teaspoon sweet pickle relish
- ½ teaspoon sugar
- ½ teaspoon distilled white vinegar
- ½ teaspoon pepper

sliders

- 12 ounces plant-based ground meat
- ¼ teaspoon table salt
- ¼ teaspoon pepper
- 8 slider hamburger buns
- 4 slices plant-based or dairy cheese (4 ounces)
- 4 teaspoons vegetable oil, divided
- ¼ cup finely chopped onion, divided
- ¼ cup water, divided

why this recipe works Sliders feature all the meaty goodness of a full-size burger concentrated into just a few bites: a juicy patty with a charred exterior embedded with chopped onion, covered in melted cheese and sandwiched in a soft steamed bun. Plant-based meat cooks through in minutes (quicker than ground beef), so we press the patties into uniform 3-inch disks to ensure that our meatless sliders all cook at the same rate. The patties are also more delicate than those made from beef, so chilling them briefly before cooking makes them easier to handle. Pressing chopped onion into the patties with a spatula helps it adhere. After flipping the patties, we top them with cheese and the bun tops, add some water to the pan, and cover it to soften the onion and melt the cheese to perfection. You can use any pie plate or baking dish to press the patties, but we prefer glass so you can see the size of the patty as you're pressing.

1 for the burger sauce: Whisk all ingredients together in bowl. (Sauce can be refrigerated for up to 4 days.)

2 for the sliders: Cut sides of 1-quart zipper-lock bag, leaving bottom seam intact. Using your moistened hands, pinch off and roll ground meat into 8 balls (1½ ounces each). Enclose 1 ball in split bag. Using clear pie plate or baking dish, press ball into even 3-inch-wide patty. Remove patty from bag and transfer to baking sheet. Repeat with remaining balls. Sprinkle patties with salt and pepper. Transfer patties to refrigerator and let chill for 15 minutes. (Patties can be refrigerated for up to 24 hours.)

3 Divide sauce evenly among bun bottoms. Arrange bun bottoms on serving platter. Stack cheese and cut into quarters (you will have 16 pieces).

4 Heat 2 teaspoons oil in 12-inch nonstick skillet over medium-high heat until just smoking. Using spatula, transfer 4 patties to skillet. Sprinkle 2 tablespoons onion evenly over tops of patties and press firmly into patties with back of spatula. Cook patties until well browned on first side, about 1 minute. Flip patties and top each with 2 pieces cheese; add bun tops. Add 2 tablespoons water to skillet (do not wet buns), cover, and continue to cook until cheese is melted, about 90 seconds.

5 Transfer sliders to prepared bun bottoms, tent with aluminum foil, and set aside while cooking remaining patties. Wipe skillet clean with paper towels. Repeat with remaining 2 teaspoons oil, remaining 4 patties, remaining 2 tablespoons onion, remaining bun tops, and remaining 2 tablespoons water. Serve.

cilantro-lime sliders with pickled cucumbers and peanut sauce

serves 8
total time 1 hour

3 tablespoons creamy
   peanut butter

4 teaspoons soy sauce, divided

5 teaspoons packed
   brown sugar, divided

2 teaspoons chili-garlic sauce

1 teaspoon grated lime zest
   plus ¼ cup juice (2 limes),
   divided

½ English cucumber, sliced thin

¼ cup thinly sliced red onion

12 ounces plant-based
   ground meat

¼ cup chopped fresh cilantro

8 slider hamburger buns

4 teaspoons vegetable oil,
   divided

why this recipe works Bite-size burgers meet outsize flavor: For a less traditional take on sliders, we bolster plant-based ground meat with fresh cilantro and lime zest. A quick chill in the fridge makes the thin patties easier to handle; set in a smoking-hot nonstick skillet, they take just over a minute to cook. As for the toppings, we slather each burger with a creamy, sweet-sour sauce whisked up using peanut butter, soy sauce, brown sugar, chili-garlic sauce, and lime juice. A quick and crunchy cucumber–red onion salad topping gives the burgers a contrasting crisp element. You can use any pie plate or baking dish to press the patties, but we prefer glass so you can see the size of the patty as you're pressing.

1 Whisk peanut butter, 2 teaspoons soy sauce, 1 tablespoon sugar, chili-garlic sauce, and 2 tablespoons lime juice in bowl until smooth; set aside. (Sauce should have consistency of ketchup; if it seems too thick, add water in small increments as needed to adjust consistency.)

2 Whisk remaining 2 teaspoons soy sauce, remaining 2 teaspoons sugar, and remaining 2 tablespoons lime juice in medium bowl until sugar has dissolved. Add cucumber and onion and toss to coat; set aside.

3 Cut sides of 1-quart zipper-lock bag, leaving bottom seam intact. Knead ground meat, cilantro, and lime zest with your hands until well combined. Using your moistened hands, pinch off and roll meat mixture into 8 balls (about 1¾ ounces each). Enclose 1 ball in split bag. Using clear pie plate or baking dish, press ball into even 3-inch-wide patty. Remove patty from bag and transfer to baking sheet. Repeat with remaining balls. Transfer patties to refrigerator and let chill for 15 minutes. (Patties can be refrigerated for up to 24 hours.)

4 Arrange bun bottoms on serving platter. Heat 2 teaspoons oil in 12-inch nonstick skillet over medium-high heat until just smoking. Using spatula, transfer 4 patties to skillet. Cook patties until well browned on first side, about 1 minute. Flip patties and cook until fully set, about 15 seconds. Transfer sliders to prepared bun bottoms, tent with aluminum foil, and set aside while cooking remaining patties. Wipe skillet clean with paper towels. Repeat with remaining 2 teaspoons oil and 4 patties. Top sliders with peanut sauce, cucumber salad, and bun tops. Serve.

jamaican meat patties

serves 8
total time 1¾ hours

filling

- 1 tablespoon vegetable oil
- 12 ounces plant-based ground meat
- 12 scallions, chopped fine
- 4 garlic cloves, minced
- 1 habanero or Scotch bonnet chile, stemmed, seeded, and minced
- 1 teaspoon dried thyme
- ¾ teaspoon curry powder
- ¾ teaspoon ground allspice
- ½ teaspoon pepper
- 1 cup water

crust

- 3 cups (15 ounces) all-purpose flour, divided
- 1 tablespoon sugar
- 1¼ teaspoons table salt
- 1 teaspoon ground turmeric
- 1 cup plus 2 tablespoons refined coconut oil, room temperature
- ½ cup ice water, plus extra as needed

why this recipe works Rich, spicy, primally satisfying ground beef hand pies are a street-food staple across the Caribbean. Since plant-based meat shines when it's layered with pungent flavors, here we create a Jamaican-inspired filling using scallions, garlic, curry powder, allspice, and chile before encasing it in golden, turmeric-infused pastry. Coconut oil makes the traditional pastry vegan-friendly. At room temperature the oil is just soft enough to pinch into small pieces that we pulse into the flour, leaving tiny pockets of fat throughout the dough. Those little pockets melt in the oven to produce a deliciously flaky crust. You'll be glad each pie is an individual serving, because once you've tasted them you won't want to share. We recommend wearing rubber gloves to protect your hands while prepping the chile; for a spicier filling, include the seeds and ribs. We prefer sweet (not hot) curry powder here. For tips on working with plant-based pie dough, see page 13.

1 for the filling: Heat oil in 12-inch nonstick skillet over medium heat until shimmering. Add ground meat and cook, breaking up meat with wooden spoon, until firm crumbles form, about 3 minutes. Stir in scallions, garlic, habanero, thyme, curry powder, allspice, and pepper and cook until scallions are softened, about 3 minutes.

2 Stir in water and bring to simmer. Cook, stirring occasionally, until sauce thickens and coats meat mixture, 5 to 7 minutes. Transfer filling to bowl and let cool completely. (Filling can be refrigerated for up to 24 hours.)

3 for the crust: Process 1½ cups flour, sugar, salt, and turmeric in food processor until combined, about 5 seconds. Pinch off ½-inch pieces of oil into flour mixture and pulse until sticky and dough just begins to clump, 12 to 15 pulses. (If mixture has paste-like consistency, chill in refrigerator until firm.) Redistribute dough around workbowl, add remaining 1½ cups flour, and pulse until just incorporated, 3 to 6 pulses; transfer to large bowl.

4 Sprinkle ice water over top of dough; then, using rubber spatula, fold and press dough to fully incorporate water and bring dough together, being careful not to overmix. If dough doesn't come together, add up to 2 tablespoons ice water, 1 teaspoon at a time. Turn out dough onto large sheet of plastic wrap and use plastic to shape into 6-inch square, smoothing any cracks. (Dough can be wrapped tightly in plastic wrap and refrigerated for up to 2 days or frozen for up to 1 month. Let dough sit at room temperature to soften completely before rolling out, about 2 hours if refrigerated or 4 hours if frozen.)

5 Adjust oven rack to upper-middle position and heat oven to 375 degrees. Line rimmed baking sheet with parchment paper. Cut dough into 4 equal pieces (about 7 ounces each); wrap each piece with plastic. Working with 1 piece at a time, sprinkle dough with flour and roll between 2 large sheets parchment paper into rough 11 by 9-inch rectangle (about ⅛ inch thick), with long side parallel to counter edge. (If dough cracks while rolling, allow it to soften further at room temperature, then pinch cracks closed and continue rolling. If dough becomes too soft, refrigerate briefly until chilled and set.) Remove parchment on top of dough.

6 Place 2 scant ⅓-cup mounds of filling on bottom half of dough, about 4 inches apart and about 2 inches from bottom edge of dough. Flatten mounds to roughly 3-inch rounds. Brush bottom half of dough lightly with water. Fold top half of dough over filling, pressing along sides, bottom edge, and between filling to adhere. Cut between mounds and trim edges to form two 5 by 4-inch rectangles. Crimp edges with floured tines of fork to seal.

7 Transfer patties to prepared sheet and bake until patties have puffed and exteriors have lightly browned, about 35 minutes. Transfer patties to wire rack and let cool for 10 minutes before serving.

albóndigas en salsa de almendras

serves 6 to 8
total time 1¼ hours

picada

- ¼ cup slivered almonds
- 1 slice hearty white sandwich bread, torn into 1-inch pieces
- 2 tablespoons extra-virgin olive oil
- 3 tablespoons minced fresh parsley
- 2 garlic cloves, minced

meatballs

- 1 slice hearty white sandwich bread, torn into 1-inch pieces
- 2 tablespoons water
- 2 tablespoons chopped fresh parsley, divided
- 2 garlic cloves, minced
- ½ teaspoon table salt
- ½ teaspoon pepper
- 12 ounces plant-based ground meat
- 1 tablespoon extra-virgin olive oil
- ½ cup finely chopped onion
- ½ teaspoon paprika
- 1 cup vegetable broth
- ½ cup dry white wine
- ¼ teaspoon saffron threads, crumbled
- 1 teaspoon sherry vinegar

why this recipe works Inspired by the Spanish tapas favorite albóndigas, these bite-size meatballs cloaked in an aromatic almond sauce are an ideal party appetizer. Adding a panade of bread and water to the meat mixture along with the garlic and parsley keeps our meat(less) balls tender by preventing their proteins from binding too tightly as they simmer in wine-enhanced broth. A nut-and-bread-based paste known as a picada thickens the sauce and adds nutty depth. And to brighten up this saucy dish, we finish with a splash of sherry vinegar and a sprinkling of fresh parsley. You can omit the saffron and increase the paprika to ¾ teaspoon, if desired. Serve with crusty bread for swiping up extra sauce.

1 for the picada: Process almonds in food processor until finely ground, about 20 seconds. Add bread and process until bread is finely ground, about 15 seconds. Transfer almond-bread mixture to 12-inch nonstick skillet. Add oil and cook over medium heat, stirring often, until mixture is golden brown, 3 to 5 minutes; transfer to bowl. Stir in parsley and garlic and set aside. Wipe skillet clean with paper towels.

2 for the meatballs: Process bread in now-empty processor until finely ground, about 15 seconds. Add water, 1 tablespoon parsley, garlic, salt, and pepper and process until evenly combined, about 20 seconds, scraping down sides of bowl as necessary. Break ground meat into small pieces and add to processor. Pulse until mixture is combined, about 10 pulses. Remove processor blade. Using your moistened hands, pinch off and roll meat mixture into generous 1-tablespoon-size meatballs and transfer to plate. Transfer meatballs to refrigerator and let chill for 15 minutes. (Meatballs can be refrigerated for up to 24 hours.)

3 Heat oil in now-empty skillet over medium heat until shimmering. Add onion and cook until softened, 4 to 6 minutes. Stir in paprika and cook until fragrant, about 30 seconds. Stir in broth and wine and bring to simmer. Stir in saffron. Gently nestle meatballs into cooking liquid. Reduce heat to medium-low, cover, and simmer until meatballs are cooked through and firm to touch, 5 to 7 minutes, flipping meatballs halfway through simmering.

4 Stir in picada and continue to cook, uncovered, until sauce has thickened slightly, about 2 minutes longer. Off heat, stir in vinegar. Season with salt and pepper to taste. Transfer meatballs to platter, sprinkle with remaining 1 tablespoon parsley, and serve.

pesto cocktail meatballs

serves 6 to 8

total time 55 minutes

4 cups fresh basil leaves

½ cup pine nuts, toasted, divided

3 garlic cloves, minced, divided

¾ teaspoon table salt, divided

5 tablespoons extra-virgin olive oil, divided

1 slice hearty white sandwich bread, torn into 1-inch pieces

12 ounces plant-based ground meat

⅛ teaspoon red pepper flakes

1 (15-ounce) can crushed tomatoes

why this recipe works Enveloped in a garlicky tomato sauce, these tender mini meatballs deliver major pesto flavor, times three. First, adding a little pesto to the meat mixture infuses the meatballs with fresh basil flavor without causing them to become too soft to hold their shape when seared. A slice of bread processed into the meat mixture binds the meatballs and keeps them moist and tender even after they're browned and cooked through; this panade is such an effective binder that there's no need to add any egg to the mix. For the second pesto addition, we stir some into the tomato sauce. Last but not least, we dollop the remaining pesto over the cooked meatballs in contrasting green mounds. A sprinkling of pine nuts adds a subtle finishing crunch. Toast the pine nuts in a dry skillet over medium-high heat until fragrant, 3 to 5 minutes. We prefer to make our own pesto here, but you can substitute ½ cup store-bought pesto, if desired; you will still need ¼ cup pine nuts for the crunchy garnish. Serve with crusty bread for swiping up extra sauce.

1 Process basil, ¼ cup pine nuts, one-third garlic, and ½ teaspoon salt in food processor until finely ground, about 30 seconds, scraping down sides of bowl as needed. With processor running, slowly add ¼ cup oil and process until smooth, about 30 seconds. Transfer pesto to bowl.

2 Process bread, 2 tablespoons pesto, and remaining ¼ teaspoon salt in now-empty processor until evenly combined, about 20 seconds, scraping down sides of bowl as needed. Break ground meat into small pieces and add to processor. Pulse until mixture is combined, about 10 pulses.

3 Remove processor blade. Using your moistened hands, pinch off and roll meat mixture into generous 1-tablespoon-size meatballs and transfer to large plate. Transfer meatballs to refrigerator and let chill for 15 minutes. (Meatballs can be refrigerated for up to 24 hours.)

4 Heat remaining 1 tablespoon oil in 12-inch nonstick skillet over medium-high heat until shimmering. Add meatballs and cook, gently turning as needed, until browned on all sides, 2 to 3 minutes. Push meatballs to side of skillet. Add pepper flakes and remaining garlic to center and cook until fragrant, about 30 seconds. Stir in tomatoes and bring to simmer.

5 Reduce heat to medium-low, cover, and simmer for 5 minutes. Off heat, stir in 3 tablespoons pesto and season with salt and pepper to taste. Transfer meatballs to platter, dollop with remaining pesto, and sprinkle with remaining ¼ cup pine nuts. Serve.

pan-fried dumplings

serves 10 to 12
(makes 40 dumplings)

total time 2 hours

12 ounces napa cabbage, cut into 1-inch pieces (5 cups)

½ teaspoon table salt

12 ounces plant-based ground meat

3 tablespoons vegetable oil, divided

1½ tablespoons soy sauce, plus extra for dipping

1½ tablespoons toasted sesame oil

1 tablespoon Shaoxing wine or dry sherry

1 tablespoon hoisin sauce

1 tablespoon grated fresh ginger

¼ teaspoon ground white pepper

4 scallions, chopped fine

40 (3½-inch) round dumpling wrappers

Black or rice vinegar

Chili oil

why this recipe works These Chinese-inspired dumplings pack amazing complexity into a small package. Instead of the fat-rich pork shoulder that's traditionally used, we start with plant-based meat, adding both vegetable oil and sesame oil to help mimic the richness of the pork; the sesame oil also brings a pleasing nutty note. Using the food processor to keep the mixing process quick and tidy, we pulse in sweet hoisin, bright Shaoxing wine, and sinus-tingling fresh ginger and white pepper. Cabbage adds contrasting crunch to the soft meat. A hybrid pan frying–steaming method cooks the dumplings until they're irresistibly crispy-chewy on the outside—perfect for dunking in little bowls of soy sauce, vinegar, and spicy chili oil. These dumplings are best served hot from the skillet; we recommend that you serve the first batch immediately and then cook the second batch. You can also serve these with the Soy-Vinegar Dipping Sauce on page 22.

1 Pulse cabbage in food processor until finely chopped, 8 to 10 pulses. Transfer cabbage to medium bowl and stir in salt; let sit for 10 minutes. Using your hands, squeeze excess moisture from cabbage. Transfer cabbage to small bowl.

2 Break ground meat into small pieces and add to now-empty processor along with 1 tablespoon vegetable oil, soy sauce, sesame oil, Shaoxing wine, hoisin, ginger, and white pepper. Pulse until mixture is combined, about 10 pulses. Scatter cabbage over meat mixture. Add scallions and pulse until vegetables are evenly distributed, about 8 pulses. Transfer meat mixture to bowl.

3 Working with 4 wrappers at a time (cover others with damp paper towel), place 1 tablespoon filling in center of each wrapper, brush edges with water, fold wrappers in half, and pinch dumplings closed, pressing out any air pockets. Place dumplings on 1 side and gently flatten bottom. Transfer to baking sheet and cover with clean, damp dish towel. (Dumplings can be frozen on baking sheet until solid, then transferred to zipper-lock bag and stored in freezer for up to 1 month. To cook from frozen, increase water in step 5 to ⅔ cup and covered cooking time to 8 minutes.)

4 Brush 1 tablespoon vegetable oil over bottom of 12-inch nonstick skillet. Evenly space 16 dumplings, flat sides down, around edge of skillet and place 4 in center (overlapping just slightly if necessary). Cook over medium heat until bottoms begin to turn spotty brown, 3 to 4 minutes.

5 Off heat, carefully add ½ cup water (water will sputter). Return skillet to heat and bring water to boil. Cover, reduce heat to medium-low, and cook for 6 minutes. Uncover, increase heat to medium-high, and cook until water has evaporated and bottoms of dumplings are crispy and browned, 1 to 3 minutes. Transfer dumplings to platter, browned sides up. (To cook second batch of dumplings, let skillet cool for 10 minutes. Rinse skillet under cool water and wipe dry with paper towels. Repeat cooking process with remaining 1 tablespoon vegetable oil and remaining dumplings.)

6 Serve dumplings hot, passing vinegar, chili oil, and extra soy sauce separately for dipping.

chapter 2
burgers, sandwiches, tacos, and more

classic burgers your way

serves 4

total time 35 minutes

1 pound plant-based ground meat

¼ teaspoon pepper

⅛ teaspoon table salt

2 teaspoons vegetable oil (if using skillet)

4 slices plant-based or dairy cheese (4 ounces) (optional)

4 hamburger buns, toasted if desired

why this recipe works These thick and juicy umami bombs are meatless burgers at their most primally satisfying. When working with beef, we like to press an indentation into the burger patties to help them cook up flat, as heat causes the meat's proteins to shrink and tighten. Plant-based meat undergoes no such shrinkage, so there's no need to indent these patties. However, we do give the shaped patties a chill in the fridge before cooking to firm them up and make them easier to handle. Starting the patties in a smoking-hot pan (or grill) yields burgers with crispy browned exteriors and juicy interiors. Dress the burgers with all your favorite toppings, or, for the purest you'll-never-believe-this-is-plant-based burger experience, just slide a patty onto a bun and dig in. This recipe will also work with four 4-ounce store-bought plant-based burger patties.

1 Using your moistened hands, divide ground meat into 4 equal portions, then gently shape each portion into 3½-inch-wide patty. Transfer patties to plate and refrigerate for at least 15 minutes or up to 24 hours. Sprinkle patties with pepper and salt.

2a for a skillet: Heat oil in 12-inch nonstick skillet over medium-high heat until just smoking. Transfer patties to skillet and cook until well browned on first side, about 3 minutes. Flip patties; top with cheese, if using; and continue to cook until browned on second side and meat registers 130 to 135 degrees, about 2 minutes longer. Serve burgers on buns.

2b for a charcoal grill: Open bottom vent completely. Light large chimney starter filled with charcoal briquettes (6 quarts). When top coals are partially covered with ash, pour evenly over grill. Set cooking grate in place, cover, and open lid vent completely. Heat grill until hot, about 5 minutes. Clean and oil cooking grate. Place patties on grill and cook until well browned on first side, about 3 minutes. Flip patties; top with cheese, if using; and continue to cook until browned on second side and meat registers 130 to 135 degrees, about 2 minutes longer. Serve burgers on buns.

2c for a gas grill: Turn all burners to high, cover, and heat grill until hot, about 15 minutes. Leave all burners on high. Clean and oil cooking grate. Place patties on grill and cook until well browned on first side, about 3 minutes. Flip patties; top with cheese, if using; and continue to cook until browned on second side and meat registers 130 to 135 degrees, about 2 minutes longer. Serve burgers on buns.

grilled smokehouse barbecue burgers

serves 4
total time 1 hour

coleslaw

- 3 cups shredded green cabbage
- 2 tablespoons sugar, plus extra for seasoning
- 1 teaspoon table salt
- 1 carrot, peeled and shredded
- 2 tablespoons cider vinegar, plus extra for seasoning
- 1 tablespoon vegetable oil
- ⅛ teaspoon celery seeds
- ⅛ teaspoon pepper

burgers

- 12 ounces plant-based ground meat
- 1 tablespoon smoked paprika
- 1 teaspoon packed brown sugar
- 1 teaspoon garlic powder
- 1 teaspoon onion powder
- ⅛ teaspoon cayenne pepper
- ⅛ teaspoon table salt
- 4 hamburger buns, toasted if desired
- ¼ cup barbecue sauce, plus extra for serving

why this recipe works Smoky. Barbecue. Burgers. Three words that are plenty appealing on their own but even more alluring together. A flaming-hot grill gives these babies terrific char marks, but because plant-based meat cooks in mere minutes, there's no time to infuse them with smokiness using a wood chip packet as we would if we were cooking with beef. Instead, the smoky flavor comes from a tablespoon of smoked paprika added to the meat. The barbecue flavors are also mixed right in: Brown sugar offers nuanced sweetness and caramelizes when exposed to heat to help the patties achieve impressive grill marks, garlic and onion powders add savory depth, and cayenne gives the burgers a kick. Topping the burgers with a slug of barbecue sauce reinforces the BBQ vibes. A quick and crunchy make-ahead coleslaw adds textural contrast to these sweet-and-savory burgers.

1 for the coleslaw: Toss cabbage with sugar and salt in large bowl. Cover and microwave, stirring occasionally, until cabbage is partially wilted and has reduced in volume by about one-third, about 2 minutes. Transfer cabbage to salad spinner and spin until excess liquid has been removed. Return cabbage to now-empty bowl; add carrot, vinegar, oil, celery seeds, and pepper; and toss to combine. Season with salt and sugar to taste. Refrigerate until well chilled, at least 30 minutes or up to 4 hours.

2 for the burgers: Break ground meat into small pieces in large bowl. Add smoked paprika, brown sugar, garlic powder, onion powder, and cayenne and gently knead with your hands until well combined. Using your moistened hands, divide meat mixture into 4 equal portions, then gently shape each portion into 3½-inch-wide patty. Transfer patties to plate and refrigerate for at least 15 minutes or up to 24 hours.

3a for a charcoal grill: Open bottom vent completely. Light large chimney starter filled with charcoal briquettes (6 quarts). When top coals are partially covered with ash, pour evenly over grill. Set cooking grate in place, cover, and open lid vent completely. Heat grill until hot, about 5 minutes.

3b for a gas grill: Turn all burners to high, cover, and heat grill until hot, about 15 minutes. Leave all burners on high.

4 Clean and oil cooking grate. Sprinkle patties with salt. Place patties on grill and cook until well browned on first side, about 3 minutes. Flip patties and continue to cook until browned on second side and meat registers 130 to 135 degrees, about 2 minutes longer.

5 Toss coleslaw to recombine. Serve burgers on buns, topped with coleslaw and 1 tablespoon barbecue sauce, passing extra barbecue sauce separately.

baharat-spiced burgers with beet tzatziki

serves 4
total time 1¼ hours

beet tzatziki

- 1 beet, peeled and shredded (¾ cup)
- ¼ English cucumber, shredded (½ cup)
- ½ teaspoon table salt
- ½ cup plain plant-based or dairy yogurt
- 2 tablespoons extra-virgin olive oil
- 1 tablespoon minced fresh mint or dill
- 1 small garlic clove, minced

burgers

- 12 ounces plant-based ground meat
- 2 teaspoons baharat
- 1½ teaspoons dried oregano
- ⅛ teaspoon table salt
- 2 teaspoons extra-virgin olive oil
- 4 hamburger buns, toasted if desired
- 1½ ounces (1½ cups) baby arugula

why this recipe works Mild plant-based meat is an ideal canvas for creative flavor combos. These burgers, made on the stovetop for ease, are a feast for both the eyes and the taste buds: toothsome patties spiked with a blend of complex, warm spices; topped with a vivid-pink, earthy-sweet beet tzatziki; and piled high with fresh, bright green arugula. Baharat, a sort of all-purpose spice blend common in Middle Eastern cuisines, comes in many iterations, but it usually includes black peppercorns, coriander, cumin, and cinnamon. Mixed right into these burger patties along with woodsy dried oregano, baharat lends its multilayered flavor to each bite. A shredded beet tinges the tangy tzatziki (a garlicky Greek cucumber-and-yogurt sauce) with its standout color, and a generous portion of baby arugula gives the burgers a peppery bite. If baharat is unavailable, substitute a combination of ¾ teaspoon cumin, ½ teaspoon pepper, ½ teaspoon ground coriander, ⅛ teaspoon ground cinnamon, and ⅛ teaspoon ground cloves.

1 for the beet tzatziki: Toss beet and cucumber with salt in colander set over medium bowl and let sit for 15 minutes. Discard any drained juices and wipe bowl clean with paper towels. Whisk yogurt, oil, mint, and garlic together in now-empty bowl, then stir in beet mixture. Cover and refrigerate for at least 1 hour or up to 24 hours. Season with salt and pepper to taste.

2 for the burgers: Break ground meat into small pieces in large bowl. Add baharat and oregano and gently knead with your hands until well combined. Using your moistened hands, divide meat mixture into 4 equal portions, then gently shape each portion into 3½-inch-wide patty. Transfer patties to plate and refrigerate for at least 15 minutes or up to 24 hours.

3 Sprinkle patties with salt. Heat oil in 12-inch nonstick skillet over medium-high heat until just smoking. Transfer patties to skillet and cook until well browned on first side, about 3 minutes. Flip patties and continue to cook until browned on second side and meat registers 130 to 135 degrees, about 2 minutes longer. Serve burgers on buns, topped with tzatziki and arugula.

italian sausage burgers with broccoli rabe and red peppers

serves 4

total time 1 hour

lemon mayonnaise

½ cup plant-based or egg-based mayonnaise

1 teaspoon grated lemon zest

1 garlic clove, minced to paste

burgers

12 ounces plant-based ground meat

1 small shallot, minced

1½ tablespoons Sweet Italian Sausage Seasoning (page 11)

4 teaspoons extra-virgin olive oil, divided

1 garlic clove, sliced thin

4 ounces broccoli rabe, trimmed and cut into ½-inch pieces

¼ cup jarred roasted red peppers, rinsed, patted dry, and sliced thin

¼ teaspoon plus ⅛ teaspoon table salt, divided

Pinch red pepper flakes

2 teaspoons light agave syrup or honey

4 hamburger buns, toasted if desired

why this recipe works Broccoli rabe probably isn't the first (or even the tenth) vegetable that comes to mind when you picture your favorite burger toppings. That's about to change. Tempered by a quick sauté in a hot pan and a drizzle of sweet agave syrup (or honey if you don't follow a vegan diet), this assertive bitter green becomes a delectable counterpoint to the rich flavors of these Italian sausage–inspired burgers. The burgers get their irresistible flavor profile from our homemade Italian seasoning blend made with fennel seeds, dried thyme, and garlic powder. The fennel seeds are key to creating that characteristic Italian pork sausage flavor, infusing the patties with their unique, faintly licorice-like taste. Jarred roasted red peppers are in keeping with the Italian theme and add a sweet vegetal element to balance the broccoli rabe's bite. A garlicky, lemony mayo adds creamy brightness. You can use store-bought mayonnaise or make our Plant-Based Mayonnaise (page 11), if desired.

1 for the lemon mayonnaise: Combine mayonnaise, lemon zest, and garlic in bowl. Refrigerate for at least 15 minutes or up to 3 days.

2 for the burgers: Break ground meat into small pieces in large bowl. Add shallot and Italian sausage seasoning and gently knead with your hands until well combined. Using your moistened hands, divide meat mixture into 4 equal portions, then gently shape each portion into 3½-inch-wide patty. Transfer patties to plate and refrigerate for at least 15 minutes or up to 24 hours.

3 Heat 2 teaspoons oil and garlic in 12-inch nonstick skillet over medium heat until garlic is golden brown and fragrant, 2 to 4 minutes. Add broccoli rabe, peppers, ¼ teaspoon salt, and pepper flakes and cook, stirring occasionally, until broccoli rabe is tender, 3 to 5 minutes. Off heat, stir in agave syrup. Transfer to bowl and cover to keep warm. Wipe skillet clean with paper towels.

4 Spread mayonnaise mixture on bun tops; set aside. Sprinkle patties with remaining ⅛ teaspoon salt. Heat remaining 2 teaspoons oil in now-empty skillet over medium-high heat until just smoking. Transfer patties to skillet and cook until well browned on first side, about 3 minutes. Flip patties and continue to cook until browned on second side and meat registers 130 to 135 degrees, about 2 minutes longer. Serve burgers on buns, topped with broccoli rabe mixture.

chorizo burgers with pineapple and poblanos

serves 4
total time 1 hour

12 ounces plant-based ground meat

¼ cup Mexican Chorizo Seasoning (page 11)

4 teaspoons extra-virgin olive oil, divided

4 (½-inch-thick) pineapple rings

1 poblano chile, stemmed, seeded, chopped fine

⅛ teaspoon table salt

¼ cup plant-based or egg-based mayonnaise

½ teaspoon lime zest plus 1 teaspoon lime juice

4 hamburger buns, toasted if desired

½ cup fresh cilantro leaves and tender stems

why this recipe works Mexican chorizo delivers flavor in spades. The exact spice mixture in chorizo varies, but you'll almost always find smoky chile, earthy cumin, oregano, and garlic. The richly spiced meat often finds its way into taco fillings (like our Chorizo and Potato Tacos with Salsa Verde on page 75), but what about a burger? Neutral-tasting plant-based meat is a great vehicle for bold spices, so for a flavor explosion in burger form, we mix our homemade chorizo seasoning right into the patties. For a sweet and fruity contrast to the spicy burgers, we sear fresh pineapple rings in a skillet until lightly caramelized. Adding a sauce is a sure-fire way to level up a burger; staying on theme, we mix up a zingy mayonnaise sauce replete with both lime zest and juice and mildly spicy fresh poblano chile. You can use store-bought mayonnaise or make our Plant-Based Mayonnaise (page 11), if desired. We prefer to use fresh pineapple rounds here, but you can substitute canned pineapple rounds, if desired.

1 Break ground meat into small pieces in large bowl. Add chorizo seasoning and gently knead with your hands until well combined. Using your moistened hands, divide meat mixture into 4 equal portions, then gently shape each portion into 3½-inch-wide patty. Transfer patties to plate and refrigerate for at least 15 minutes or up to 24 hours.

2 Heat 1 teaspoon oil in 12-inch nonstick skillet over medium-high heat until shimmering. Pat pineapple dry with paper towels, then add to skillet and cook until softened and lightly charred, about 3 minutes per side. Transfer to plate and set aside. Add poblano and 1 teaspoon oil to now-empty skillet and cook until softened, about 3 minutes. Transfer to medium bowl and set aside.

3 Sprinkle patties with salt. Heat remaining 2 teaspoons oil in now-empty skillet over medium-high heat until just smoking. Transfer patties to skillet and cook until well browned on first side, about 3 minutes. Flip patties and continue to cook until browned on second side and meat registers 130 to 135 degrees, about 2 minutes longer.

4 Stir mayonnaise and lime zest and juice into poblano and season with salt and pepper to taste. Spread poblano mixture on bun tops and bun bottoms and top with burgers, pineapple, cilantro, and bun tops. Serve.

meatloaf burgers with crispy smashed tater tots

serves 4
total time 50 minutes

¼ cup ketchup

1 tablespoon packed brown sugar

1 teaspoon cider vinegar

12 ounces plant-based ground meat

2 teaspoons soy sauce

1 teaspoon minced fresh thyme

½ teaspoon pepper

2 teaspoons plus 1½ tablespoons vegetable oil, divided

1 cup frozen tater tots, thawed and patted dry

4 hamburger buns, toasted if desired

why this recipe works The comforting flavors of meatloaf get a modern update in these meatless, loaf-less, undeniably charming burgers. We slather the tender patties with a sweet tomatoey glaze and, in a whimsical nod to the mashed potatoes so often served as part of a classic meatloaf dinner, we top each burger with smashed and pan-fried tater tots. The crispy, crunchy tater tot topping couldn't be easier—we just thaw a handful of store-bought tots before pressing them into the same pan we use to cook the burgers. As for the patties themselves, mixing some earthy, savory fresh thyme into the plant-based meat gets us on the right flavor path, and a splash of soy sauce adds umami depth. To drive the meatloaf flavor home, we mix up a traditional glaze of ketchup, brown sugar, and cider vinegar (why mess with perfection?); brush a portion of this liquid magic directly onto the cooked patties; and reserve the rest for spreading over the bun tops. Serve with your favorite burger toppings.

1 Whisk ketchup, sugar, and vinegar in bowl until combined.

2 Break ground meat into small pieces in large bowl. Add soy sauce, thyme, and pepper and gently knead with your hands until well combined. Using your moistened hands, divide meat mixture into 4 equal portions, then gently shape each portion into 3½-inch-wide patty. Transfer patties to plate and refrigerate for at least 15 minutes or up to 24 hours.

3 Heat 2 teaspoons oil in 12-inch nonstick skillet over medium-high heat until just smoking. Transfer patties to skillet and cook until well browned on first side, about 3 minutes. Flip patties and continue to cook until browned on second side and meat registers 130 to 135 degrees, about 2 minutes. Transfer burgers to platter and brush with ketchup mixture.

4 Heat remaining 1½ tablespoons oil in now-empty skillet over medium-high heat until shimmering. Add tater tots to skillet and press with spatula or underside of dry measuring cup to flatten slightly. Cook until crispy and deep golden brown, about 4 minutes per side. Transfer tater tots to paper towel–lined plate.

5 Spread remaining ketchup mixture evenly over each bun top. Top burgers with tater tots and serve burgers on buns.

double smashie burgers

serves 4
total time 1 hour

burger sauce

- ¼ cup plant-based or egg-based mayonnaise
- 2 tablespoons ketchup
- 1 teaspoon sweet pickle relish
- 1 teaspoon sugar
- 1 teaspoon distilled white vinegar
- ½ teaspoon pepper

burgers

- 12 ounces plant-based ground meat
- 4 hamburger buns, toasted if desired
- 1½ cups shredded iceberg lettuce
- ¼ teaspoon table salt
- ¼ teaspoon pepper
- 1 tablespoon vegetable oil
- 4 slices plant-based or dairy cheese (4 ounces)
- ¼ cup finely chopped onion
- ¼ cup dill pickle chips

why this recipe works There's a reason beyond mere convenience why fast-food burgers are so beloved—it's the particular combination of salty, crispy, sweet, sour, pickled, savory, and meaty that fast-food chains do so well. Here, we use plant-based meat to replicate that ultimate fast-food-style burger patty: pressed thin and deeply browned to crispy deliciousness. Cooking the patties in a blazing-hot skillet triggers the Maillard reaction, a process (signaled by browning) that causes the proteins and sugars in food to recombine and form hundreds of new flavor compounds. The result: super savory, drool-worthy burgers. To aid in the browning, we weight the patties with a heavy Dutch oven to ensure maximum contact with the hot pan. And since each patty is so thin, we double them up for twice the impact and a heftier burger overall. The rest is just a matter of slathering on the superquick fast food–style burger sauce and layering with your favorite burger toppings. Order's up! You can use any pie plate or baking dish to press the patties, but we prefer glass so you can see the size of the patty as you're pressing.

1 for the burger sauce: Whisk all ingredients together in bowl. (Sauce can be refrigerated for up to 4 days.)

2 for the burgers: Wrap bottom of Dutch oven with aluminum foil. Cut sides of 1-quart zipper-lock bag, leaving bottom seam intact.

3 Using your moistened hands, pinch off and roll ground meat into 8 balls (1½ ounces each). Enclose 1 ball in split bag. Using clear pie plate or baking dish, press ball into even 3½-inch-wide patty. Remove patty from bag and transfer to baking sheet. Repeat with remaining balls. Transfer patties to refrigerator and let chill for at least 15 minutes or up to 24 hours.

4 Spread 1 tablespoon burger sauce over each bun bottom, then top with lettuce; set aside. Sprinkle patties with salt and pepper. Heat oil in 12-inch nonstick skillet over high heat until just smoking. Using spatula, transfer 4 patties to skillet and weight with prepared pot. Cook patties until well browned on first side, about 1 minute. Remove pot, flip patties, and top with cheese. Cook until patties are just cooked through, about 15 seconds. Transfer patties to prepared bun bottoms.

5 Repeat with remaining 4 patties. Stack patties and top with onion, pickle chips, and bun tops. Serve, passing remaining burger sauce separately.

larb lettuce wraps with lime, mint, and cilantro

serves 4
total time 40 minutes

1 tablespoon white rice

¼ cup vegetable broth

12 ounces plant-based ground meat

2 shallots, sliced thin

3 tablespoons lime juice (2 limes)

4 tablespoons coarsely chopped fresh mint

4 tablespoons coarsely chopped fresh cilantro

2 teaspoons sugar

¼ teaspoon red pepper flakes

2 tablespoons soy sauce

1 head Bibb lettuce (8 ounces), leaves separated

why this recipe works A lettuce wrap is a light and fresh choice for dinner, and this one is a cause for real excitement. It takes its inspiration from larb moo, a sweet-spicy-savory Thai meat salad made with minced pork and lots of fresh herbs. Here, our meaty crumbled filling is perked up with lots of fresh mint and cilantro, lime juice, and umami-packed soy sauce. Unlike with animal meat, there's no need to salt plant-based meat (which already contains some sodium) prior to searing it. Less flashy but no less important than the meat is the toasted rice powder, or koa kua, which is integral to the texture and flavor of the dish and can be made in minutes from regular white rice. An essential ingredient in traditional larb moo, it helps thicken the moist filling and gives the fresh, bright wraps a distinct, balancing nuttiness. Any style of white rice can be used. You can use 1 tablespoon of store-bought toasted rice powder (koa kua) instead of making your own; look for it in stores that carry Thai ingredients. For a heartier meal, serve with sticky rice and steamed vegetables.

1 Toast rice in 8-inch skillet over medium-high heat, stirring constantly, until deep golden brown, about 5 minutes. Transfer rice to small bowl and let cool for 5 minutes. Grind to fine meal using spice grinder, mini food processor, or mortar and pestle, 10 to 30 seconds (you should have about 1 tablespoon rice powder).

2 Bring broth to simmer in 12-inch nonstick skillet over medium-high heat. Add ground meat and cook, breaking up meat with wooden spoon, until firm crumbles begin to form, about 1 minute. Sprinkle 1 teaspoon rice powder into skillet and continue to cook until crumbles are fully set, 1 to 2 minutes.

3 Transfer meat mixture to large bowl and let cool for 10 minutes. Stir in shallots, lime juice, mint, cilantro, sugar, pepper flakes, soy sauce, and remaining 2 teaspoons rice powder and toss to combine. Serve with lettuce leaves.

pita sandwiches with cucumber-yogurt sauce

serves 4
total time 1¼ hours

¾ cup plain plant-based or dairy yogurt

½ cucumber, peeled, halved lengthwise, seeded, and chopped fine

2 tablespoons lemon juice, divided

3 garlic cloves, minced to paste, divided

1 tablespoon minced fresh mint or dill

½ teaspoon table salt, divided

4 (8-inch) pita breads

½ onion, chopped coarse

1 tablespoon minced fresh oregano or 1 teaspoon dried

1 teaspoon ground cumin

¼ teaspoon pepper

12 ounces plant-based ground meat

2 teaspoons vegetable oil

1 large tomato, sliced thin

2 cups shredded lettuce

why this recipe works A traditional Greek gyro starts with cooking seasoned meat on a vertical rotisserie for hours. Since most home cooks don't have that kind of setup, a while back we developed a simplified recipe that calls for shaping the meat into patties and cooking them in a skillet. That's the recipe we used as the jumping-off point for these plant-based gyro-style pitas. To keep the patties moist, we borrow the idea of using a panade (a paste of bread and water) from our plant-based meatball recipes, using pita scraps as the bread. To complete the pitas, we stuff them with sliced tomato and shredded lettuce and make a cooling cucumber-yogurt sauce. If using pocketless pitas, heat them in a single layer on a baking sheet in a 350-degree oven for 5 minutes. Do not cut the top quarters off pocketless pitas; instead, use a portion of a fifth pita to create the pieces in step 2.

1 Combine yogurt, cucumber, 1 tablespoon lemon juice, ½ teaspoon garlic, mint, and ¼ teaspoon salt in bowl. Cover and refrigerate until ready to serve. (Sauce can be refrigerated for up to 24 hours.)

2 Cut top quarter off each pita bread. Tear 1 top quarter into 1-inch pieces and discard remaining 3 top quarters. (You should have about ¼ cup pita pieces.) Stack pitas and wrap tightly in aluminum foil; set aside.

3 Process onion, oregano, cumin, pepper, pita pieces, remaining 1 tablespoon lemon juice, remaining garlic, and remaining ¼ teaspoon salt in food processor until mixture forms a cohesive paste, about 30 seconds, scraping down sides of bowl as needed. Add ground meat and pulse until combined, about 10 pulses. Remove processor blade. Using your moistened hands, divide meat mixture into 12 lightly packed balls, then flatten into ½-inch-thick patties. Transfer patties to plate and refrigerate for at least 15 minutes or up to 24 hours.

4 Adjust oven rack to middle position and heat oven to 350 degrees. Place foil-wrapped pitas directly on oven rack and heat for 10 minutes. Meanwhile, heat oil in 12-inch nonstick skillet over medium-high heat until just smoking. Using spatula, transfer patties to skillet and cook until well browned on first side, about 3 minutes. Flip patties and continue to cook until browned on second side and meat registers 130 to 135 degrees, about 2 minutes longer. Divide patties, tomato, and lettuce among pitas and serve, passing sauce separately.

grilled kofte wraps

serves 4

total time 1 hour

yogurt-tahini sauce

- 1 cup plain plant-based or dairy yogurt
- 2 tablespoons lemon juice
- 2 tablespoons tahini
- 1 garlic clove, minced to paste
- ¼ teaspoon table salt

kofte

- 1 small red onion (½ chopped, ½ sliced thin)
- ½ cup panko bread crumbs
- ¼ cup pine nuts
- 3 tablespoons chopped fresh parsley
- 3 tablespoons chopped fresh mint
- 2 tablespoons water
- 3 garlic cloves, peeled
- 1 teaspoon hot smoked paprika
- 1 teaspoon ground cumin
- ¼ teaspoon pepper
- ⅛ teaspoon ground coriander
- ⅛ teaspoon ground cloves
- ⅛ teaspoon table salt
- 12 ounces plant-based ground meat
- 4 (8-inch) pita breads
- 1 large tomato, sliced thin
- 2 cups shredded lettuce

why this recipe works Throughout the Middle East, kebabs called kofte are made by mixing ground beef with delightfully extravagant quantities of fresh herbs and warm spices. The beef mixture—formed around skewers, rolled into logs, or pressed into patties, depending on region and personal preference—is grilled over high heat and served with a creamy yogurt sauce. Since the protein composition in plant-based meat makes it more delicate than beef, our plant-based kofte were prone to breaking apart on the grill when formed onto skewers. Doing away with the skewers and rolling the kofte into logs allows us to handle them more gently with tongs, so they're less apt to crumble. (A well-oiled grill grate helps, too.) The tangy yogurt-tahini sauce cuts through the koftes' richness and spice, and red onion, tomato, and shredded lettuce add a fresh, crisp touch. The intense heat of a charcoal fire mimics that of a kofte grill, but you can use a gas grill instead. If you like, serve the kofte with a side of rice pilaf rather than making wraps.

1 for the yogurt-tahini sauce: Whisk all ingredients together in bowl. Cover and refrigerate until ready to serve. (Sauce can be refrigerated for up to 24 hours.)

2 for the kofte: Process chopped onion, panko, pine nuts, parsley, mint, water, garlic, paprika, cumin, pepper, coriander, cloves, and salt in food processor until mixture forms a cohesive paste, about 30 seconds, scraping down sides of bowl as needed. Add ground meat and pulse to combine, about 10 pulses.

3 Remove processor blade. Using your moistened hands, divide meat mixture into 4 equal portions. Shape each portion into 4½-inch-long cylinder about 1 inch in diameter. Transfer kofte to plate and refrigerate for at least 15 minutes or up to 24 hours.

4 Lightly moisten 2 pita breads with water. Sandwich 2 unmoistened pita breads between moistened pita breads and wrap stack tightly in lightly greased heavy-duty aluminum foil.

5a for a charcoal grill: Open bottom vent completely. Light large chimney starter filled with charcoal briquettes (6 quarts). When top coals are partially covered with ash, pour evenly over grill. Set cooking grate in place, cover, and open lid vent completely. Heat grill until hot, about 5 minutes.

5b for a gas grill: Turn all burners to high, cover, and heat grill until hot, about 15 minutes. Leave all burners on high.

6 Clean and oil cooking grate. Place kofte on grill perpendicular to grate bars. Cook (covered if using gas) until well browned on first side, about 3 minutes. Flip kofte and continue to cook until browned on second side and meat registers 130 to 135 degrees, about 2 minutes longer. Transfer kofte to plate.

7 Meanwhile, place packet of pitas on grill and cook, flipping occasionally, until heated through, about 5 minutes. Lay each warm pita on 12-inch square of foil. Spread each pita with 2 tablespoons sauce. Place 1 kofte in middle of each pita and top with tomato, lettuce, and sliced onion. Roll into cylindrical shape and serve, passing remaining sauce separately.

meat-lover's veggie banh mi

serves 4

total time 1 hour

¼ cup unseasoned rice vinegar

2 tablespoons soy sauce, divided

1 teaspoon sugar

¼ teaspoon table salt

3 carrots, peeled and cut into 2-inch matchsticks

½ English cucumber, cut into 2-inch matchsticks

1 cup fresh cilantro leaves and tender stems, divided

½ cup panko bread crumbs

4 scallions, white parts chopped, green parts sliced thin

1 tablespoon water

1 tablespoon sriracha, divided

2 teaspoons grated lime zest, divided

12 ounces plant-based ground meat

2 teaspoons vegetable oil

½ cup plant-based or egg-based mayonnaise

2 (12-inch) baguettes, ends trimmed, halved crosswise, and split lengthwise

why this recipe works A popular Vietnamese street food, banh mi are exquisite hybrids of Vietnamese and French cuisine. Typically they contain pickled vegetables, chiles, cilantro, mayonnaise, and protein (often marinated pork and/or pâté), all cradled within a crusty split baguette. Plant-based versions often rely on tofu, but here we turn to succulent and savory plant-based meat. We season the meat with soy sauce, scallion whites, lime zest, cilantro, and a touch of spicy sriracha, stir in bread crumbs to help it retain moisture when cooked, and then form the mixture into patties. The flattened sides give tons of surface area for picking up flavorful browning. The crisp, tangy vegetable element (here, carrots and cucumber) can be quick-pickled in a mere 15 minutes. For an intense finishing touch, we whip up a quick mayonnaise sauce spiked with more sriracha and lime zest. You can use store-bought mayonnaise or make our Plant-Based Mayonnaise (page 11), if desired.

1 Microwave vinegar, 1 tablespoon soy sauce, sugar, and salt in large bowl until steaming, about 2 minutes. Stir in carrots and cucumber and let sit, tossing occasionally, for at least 15 minutes or up to 1 hour. Drain vegetables and return to bowl. (Pickled vegetables can be refrigerated for up to 24 hours.)

2 Process ½ cup cilantro, panko, scallion whites, water, ½ teaspoon sriracha, 1 teaspoon lime zest, and remaining 1 tablespoon soy sauce in food processor until mixture forms cohesive paste, about 30 seconds, scraping down sides of bowl as needed. Add ground meat and pulse to combine, about 10 pulses. Remove processor blade. Using your moistened hands, divide meat mixture into 12 lightly packed balls, then flatten into ½-inch-thick patties. Transfer patties to plate and refrigerate for at least 15 minutes or up to 24 hours.

3 Heat oil in 12-inch nonstick skillet over medium-high heat until just smoking. Using spatula, transfer patties to skillet and cook until well browned on first side, about 3 minutes. Flip patties and continue to cook until browned on second side and meat registers 130 to 135 degrees, about 2 minutes longer.

4 Stir scallion greens into pickled vegetables. Whisk mayonnaise, remaining 2½ teaspoons sriracha, and remaining 1 teaspoon lime zest together in bowl. Spread mayonnaise mixture evenly over cut sides of baguette. Layer patties, pickled vegetables, and remaining ½ cup cilantro evenly over bottom halves. Top with baguette tops and serve.

italian meatball subs
with broccoli

serves 4
total time 1¼ hours

½ cup panko bread crumbs

2 tablespoons water

½ teaspoon garlic powder

½ teaspoon table salt, divided

¼ teaspoon pepper, divided

⅛ teaspoon dried oregano

12 ounces plant-based ground meat

1 head broccoli (1½ pounds)

2 tablespoons extra-virgin olive oil, plus extra for drizzling

½ teaspoon sugar

4 (6-inch) Italian sub rolls, split partially lengthwise

8 slices plant-based or dairy cheese (8 ounces)

1⅓ cups jarred marinara sauce

2 teaspoons lemon juice

why this recipe works Here's some appealing kitchen math: a main plus a side plus just one dirty pan and bowl to wash, all multiplied by comforting, crowd-pleasing flavor. The subjects of our little equation are these saucy subs. We knead the meat with panko bread crumbs (to bind and tenderize the meatballs) and Italian-inspired seasonings, roll it into balls, and then pop the meatballs into the oven on a rimmed baking sheet, avoiding the splattery mess that comes with stovetop simmering. Bonus: There's enough room on the sheet to roast a simple side of broccoli simultaneously. We cut the broccoli into large wedges for visual drama and toss it with oil and a sprinkling of sugar to yield deep caramelization by the time the meatballs are cooked through. To gild the lily, we melt a couple slices of cheese (either plant-based or dairy-based) onto the sub rolls before assembling our sandwiches. We prefer to make our own meatballs, but you can substitute twelve 1-ounce store-bought plant-based meatballs, if desired. If using store-bought meatballs, make sure they are completely thawed and skip step 1.

1 Stir panko, water, garlic powder, ¼ teaspoon salt, ⅛ teaspoon pepper, and oregano in large bowl until mixture forms cohesive paste. Break ground meat into small pieces and add to bowl with panko mixture. Gently knead with your hands until mixture is well combined. Using your moistened hands, pinch off and roll meat mixture into 12 meatballs. Transfer meatballs to plate and refrigerate for at least 15 minutes or up to 24 hours.

2 Adjust oven rack to middle position and heat oven to 475 degrees. Grease aluminum foil–lined rimmed baking sheet. Cut broccoli at juncture of florets and stems; remove outer peel from stalk. Cut stalk into ½-inch-thick planks, 2 to 3 inches long. Cut crowns into 4 wedges if 3 to 4 inches in diameter or 6 wedges if 4 to 5 inches in diameter. Toss broccoli with oil, sugar, remaining ¼ teaspoon salt, and remaining ⅛ teaspoon pepper. Arrange meatballs evenly on 1 half of prepared sheet. Lay broccoli cut side down on opposite side of sheet from meatballs. Roast until meatballs are firm and cooked through, 8 to 10 minutes.

3 Transfer meatballs to plate and return sheet to oven. Continue to roast broccoli until tender, about 5 minutes. Transfer broccoli to serving platter. Discard foil.

4 Place rolls on now-empty sheet with open sides facing up and place 2 slices of cheese inside each roll. Bake until cheese is melted and roll is toasted, 4 to 5 minutes. Arrange 3 meatballs in each roll and top with ⅓ cup marinara sauce. Drizzle broccoli with lemon juice and extra oil. Serve meatball subs with broccoli.

bratwurst sandwiches with red potato and kale salad

serves 4

total time 50 minutes

1 pound small red potatoes, unpeeled, halved

7 tablespoons extra-virgin olive oil, divided

1 teaspoon table salt, divided

½ teaspoon pepper, divided

2 red onions, halved and sliced ¼ inch thick

4 (3½-ounce) plant-based bratwurst sausages

¼ cup whole-grain mustard, divided, plus extra for serving

2 tablespoons red wine vinegar

4 hot dog buns, toasted if desired

5 ounces (5 cups) baby kale

4 radishes, trimmed and sliced thin

why this recipe works Two are better than one, the saying goes, so here's another great sheet-pan meal to keep in your cooking arsenal for busy weeknights. This one features hearty sausage sandwiches and a tangy potato-kale salad ready in under an hour. Plant-based bratwurst steals the show and requires zero prep: We simply roast the brats on a rimmed baking sheet alongside sliced red onions and some halved red potatoes. The hands-off cooking time lets us focus on the side salad—which also comes together amazingly quickly. We whisk together a zippy dressing of extra-virgin olive oil, red wine vinegar, and whole-grain mustard and then toss it with baby kale and the roasted potatoes. We then nestle the brats and onions in toasted hot dog buns, dish up the warm potato salad, and dig in. Just like that, dinner is done. Look for red potatoes that are 1 to 2 inches in diameter. We prefer the flavor of bratwurst-style sausages here, but any style of plant-based sausage will work.

1 Adjust oven rack to middle position, place rimmed baking sheet on rack, and heat oven to 425 degrees. Toss potatoes with 2 tablespoons oil, ½ teaspoon salt, and ¼ teaspoon pepper in bowl; arrange cut side down on 1 half of prepared sheet.

2 Toss onions with 1 tablespoon oil in now-empty bowl. Place sausages on opposite side of sheet from potatoes, then scatter onions around sausages. Roast until potatoes are tender and sausages are fully cooked, 25 to 30 minutes, flipping sausages halfway through roasting.

3 Whisk 2 tablespoons mustard, vinegar, remaining ¼ cup oil, remaining ½ teaspoon salt, and remaining ¼ teaspoon pepper together in large bowl. Remove sheet from oven. Add potatoes to bowl with dressing and toss to coat.

4 Divide sausages and onions evenly among buns and top with remaining 2 tablespoons mustard. Add kale and radishes to potatoes and toss to combine. Season with salt and pepper to taste. Serve sandwiches with potato salad, passing extra mustard separately.

breakfast sausage sandwiches

<table>
<tr><td>serves 4</td></tr>
<tr><td>total time 40 minutes</td></tr>
</table>

8 ounces plant-based ground meat

1 tablespoon Breakfast Sausage Seasoning (page 10)

2 teaspoons vegetable oil

¼ cup Cashew Ricotta with Roasted Red Peppers (page 12)

4 English muffins, split and lightly toasted

1 cup (1 ounce) watercress, torn into bite-size pieces

1 tomato, cored and sliced thin

why this recipe works Any day that starts off with a savory breakfast sandwich is already looking up. This highly customizable breakfast food can go in nearly any flavor direction: Here, we keep it simple yet elevated with a schmear of roasted red pepper cashew ricotta; a toasted English muffin; ripe, juicy tomato slices; and a handful of peppery watercress—plus, of course, the requisite sausage patty made of plant-based meat. For sausage identity, we mix plant-based meat with our breakfast sausage seasoning mix, which includes garlic powder, brown sugar, dried sage, and dried thyme. The uncooked patties can be frozen to give you a head start on several days' breakfast; just cook them from frozen when you're ready. Alternatively, you can freeze the cooked patties and reheat them as needed in the microwave. We prefer to make our own breakfast patties, but you can substitute four 1½-ounce store-bought plant-based breakfast patties, if desired. If using store-bought patties, make sure they are completely thawed and skip step 1. You can substitute plain store-bought plant-based ricotta or dairy ricotta for the cashew ricotta, if desired.

1 Break ground meat into small pieces in large bowl. Add seasoning and gently knead with your hands until well combined. Using your moistened hands, divide meat mixture into 4 lightly packed balls, then flatten into ½-inch-thick patties. Transfer patties to plate and refrigerate for at least 15 minutes or up to 24 hours.

2 Heat oil in 12-inch nonstick skillet over medium-high heat until just smoking. Using spatula, transfer patties to skillet and cook until well browned on first side, about 3 minutes. Flip patties and continue to cook until browned on second side and meat registers 130 to 135 degrees, about 2 minutes longer. Spread ricotta on muffin bottoms. Layer patties, watercress, and tomato over bottom halves. Top with muffin tops. Serve.

variation breakfast sausage sandwiches with fried eggs

Transfer patties to plate after cooking and wipe skillet clean with paper towels. Heat 1 tablespoon oil in now-empty skillet over medium heat until shimmering. Meanwhile, crack up to 4 eggs into bowl and sprinkle with pinch salt and pinch pepper. Once oil is shimmering, pour eggs into skillet; cover and cook until whites are cooked and yolk is to your liking, 3 to 5 minutes. To serve, layer eggs with patties and remaining toppings.

breakfast tacos

serves 4 to 6

total time 50 minutes, plus 20 minutes draining

salsa roja

1 pound plum tomatoes, cored and chopped

2 garlic cloves, chopped

1 jalapeño chile, stemmed, seeded, and chopped

2 tablespoons chopped fresh cilantro

1 tablespoon lime juice

1 teaspoon table salt

¼ teaspoon red pepper flakes

tacos

14 ounces soft tofu

2 tablespoons vegetable oil

2 green bell peppers, stemmed, seeded, and chopped fine

1 onion, chopped fine

1 jalapeño chile, stemmed, seeded, and minced

½ teaspoon table salt

8 ounces plant-based ground meat

1 tablespoon ground cumin

1 teaspoon chili powder

2 garlic cloves, minced

12 (6-inch) flour tortillas, warmed

Lime wedges

why this recipe works In southern Texas, tacos are fair game at breakfast as well as at lunch and dinner. We think even Texans would love our plant-based take on their famous breakfast (or anytime) tacos. Eggs are a breakfast taco mainstay; to make our tacos vegan-friendly, we get creative with soft tofu, breaking it into irregularly sized pieces to mimic egg curds. Cumin, chili powder, and garlic give crumbled plant-based meat a subtle spiciness that pops next to the mild, creamy tofu. A south Texas–inspired cooked tomato salsa with jalapeño, cilantro, and lime juice wakes you up with a wallop of freshness and spice. You can substitute silken tofu for the soft tofu, but your scramble will be significantly wetter. Do not use firm tofu. For a spicier salsa, reserve and add the jalapeño ribs and seeds to the blender before processing. Level up these tacos by serving them with sliced radishes, chopped avocado, and fresh cilantro.

1 for the salsa roja: Combine tomatoes and garlic in bowl and microwave, uncovered, until steaming and liquid begins to pool in bottom of bowl, about 4 minutes. Transfer tomato mixture to fine-mesh strainer set over bowl and let drain for 5 minutes.

2 Process jalapeño, cilantro, lime juice, salt, pepper flakes, and tomato mixture in blender until smooth, about 45 seconds, scraping down sides of blender jar as needed. Season with salt to taste. (Salsa can be refrigerated for up to 3 days. Cover and microwave briefly to rewarm before serving.)

3 for the tacos: Crumble tofu into ¼- to ½-inch pieces. Spread tofu on paper towel–lined baking sheet and let drain for 20 minutes, then gently press dry with paper towels.

4 Heat oil in 12-inch nonstick skillet over medium heat until shimmering. Add bell peppers, onion, jalapeño, and salt and cook until softened and lightly browned, 5 to 7 minutes. Add ground meat, cumin, chili powder, and garlic and cook, breaking up meat with wooden spoon, until firm crumbles form, about 3 minutes. Stir in tofu and cook until heated through, about 2 minutes. Divide filling evenly among tortillas and serve, passing salsa and lime wedges separately.

variation breakfast tacos with scrambled eggs

Omit tofu. After firm meat crumbles form in step 4, add 6 lightly beaten eggs and cook, using spatula to constantly and firmly scrape along bottom and sides of skillet, until eggs begin to clump and spatula leaves trail on bottom of skillet, 1½ to 2½ minutes. Reduce heat to low. Gently but constantly fold egg mixture until clumped and slightly wet, 30 to 60 seconds. Serve as directed.

not-from-a-box weeknight tacos

serves 4 to 6
total time 35 minutes

1 tablespoon vegetable oil

1 onion, chopped fine

1 green bell pepper, stemmed, seeded, and chopped fine

½ teaspoon table salt

4 garlic cloves, minced

1 tablespoon chili powder

1 teaspoon ground cumin

½ teaspoon pepper

¼ teaspoon cayenne pepper (optional)

2 tablespoons tomato paste

12 ounces plant-based ground meat

½ cup water

12 (6-inch) corn tortillas, warmed

why this recipe works Meaty tacos piled high with fresh toppings always disappear from the table in a flash. A few tweaks to our everyday ground beef taco recipe transform this family favorite into a plant-based feast. Our ground beef taco recipe calls for adding the meat to the skillet before the aromatics to give it a head start, but plant-based meat cooks so quickly that we find it best to reverse the usual order. First, we add the aromatics to the oil and cook them until softened, and then we bloom the spices and stir in tomato paste, adding the plant-based meat to the skillet for only the last few minutes. This method browns the meat but also keeps it supple and moist, not pebbly. Finishing the filling by simmering it with a splash of water gives it a delightfully saucy consistency. The spice level of chili powder varies greatly by brand; we like a little heat in our tacos, but if you don't or you're unsure of how spicy your chili powder is, feel free to omit the cayenne. Serve with your favorite taco toppings.

1 Heat oil in 12-inch nonstick skillet over medium heat until shimmering. Add onion, bell pepper, and salt and cook until softened and lightly browned, 5 to 7 minutes.

2 Stir in garlic; chili powder; cumin; pepper; and cayenne, if using, and cook until fragrant, about 30 seconds. Stir in tomato paste and cook until rust-colored, 1 to 2 minutes.

3 Stir in ground meat and cook, breaking up meat with wooden spoon, until firm crumbles form, about 3 minutes. Stir in water and simmer until sauce is thickened, about 1 minute. Divide filling evenly among tortillas and serve.

crispy fried tacos with almonds and raisins

<table>
<tr><td>serves 4 to 6</td></tr>
<tr><td>total time 1¼ hours</td></tr>
</table>

7 tablespoons extra-virgin olive oil, divided

1 small onion, chopped fine

2 garlic cloves, minced

½ teaspoon minced canned chipotle chile in adobo sauce

½ teaspoon ground cinnamon

⅛ teaspoon ground cloves

12 ounces plant-based ground meat

1 cup vegetable broth

½ cup canned tomato sauce

2 tablespoons chopped raisins

1 tablespoon cider vinegar

½ teaspoon table salt

½ teaspoon pepper

¼ cup slivered almonds, toasted

12 (6-inch) corn tortillas

why this recipe works Is it really taco night if you don't have a trail of spice-infused oil running down your arm after biting into a shatteringly crispy taco shell? These tacos are a mash-up inspired by two classics: tacos dorados (crispy fried beef-filled tacos) and tacos de picadillo Oaxaqueño (ground pork tacos with onions, raisins, and warm spices). As with our Not-from-a-Box Weeknight Tacos (page 71), we soften the onion and bloom the spices in oil before adding the plant-based meat. Raisins and almonds take the filling from everyday to extraordinary, adding richness and pops of sweetness. We then stuff corn tortillas with the filling and shallow-fry them until crispy. Don't worry—the cohesive filling won't fall out of the unsealed shells. In fact, the filling's moisture keeps the shells' folded middles pliable so the tacos don't crack down the center at first bite. Arrange the tacos so that they face the same direction in the skillet to make them easy to fit and flip. To ensure crispy tacos, cook the tortillas until they are deeply browned. To garnish, open each taco like a book and load it with your favorite toppings. Then fold it back up and devour.

1 Adjust oven rack to middle position and heat oven to 400 degrees. Heat 1 tablespoon oil in 12-inch nonstick skillet over medium heat until shimmering. Add onion and cook until softened, about 5 minutes. Stir in garlic, chipotle, cinnamon, and cloves and cook until fragrant, about 30 seconds. Add ground meat and cook, breaking up meat with wooden spoon, until firm crumbles form, about 3 minutes.

2 Stir in broth, tomato sauce, raisins, vinegar, salt, and pepper and simmer until sauce is thickened, about 5 minutes. Stir in almonds and season with salt and pepper to taste. Transfer meat filling to bowl; wipe skillet clean with paper towels.

3 Thoroughly brush both sides of tortillas with 2 tablespoons oil. Arrange tortillas, overlapping, on rimmed baking sheet in 2 rows (6 tortillas each). Bake until tortillas are warm and pliable, about 5 minutes. Remove tortillas from oven and reduce oven temperature to 200 degrees.

4 Place 3 tablespoons filling on 1 side of 1 tortilla. Fold and press to close tortilla (edges will be open, but tortilla will remain folded). Repeat with remaining tortillas and remaining filling. (Filled tortillas can be covered and refrigerated for up to 12 hours.)

5 Set wire rack in second rimmed baking sheet and line rack with double layer of paper towels. Heat remaining ¼ cup oil in now-empty skillet over medium-high heat until shimmering. Arrange 6 tacos in skillet with open sides facing away from you. Cook, adjusting heat so oil actively sizzles and bubbles appear around edges of tacos, until tacos are crispy and deeply browned on 1 side, 2 to 3 minutes. Using tongs and thin spatula, carefully flip tacos. Cook until deeply browned on second side, 2 to 3 minutes, adjusting heat as necessary.

6 Remove skillet from heat and transfer tacos to prepared wire rack. Blot tops of tacos with double layer of paper towels. Place sheet with fried tacos in oven to keep warm. Return skillet to medium-high heat and cook remaining tacos. Serve.

chorizo and potato tacos
with salsa verde

serves 4 to 6

total time 1 hour

salsa verde

8 ounces tomatillos, husks and stems removed, rinsed well, dried, and cut into 1-inch pieces

1 avocado, halved, pitted, and cut into 1-inch pieces

1–2 jalapeño chiles, stemmed, seeded, and chopped

¼ cup chopped fresh cilantro

1 tablespoon lime juice

1 garlic clove, minced

¾ teaspoon table salt

filling

1 pound Yukon Gold potatoes, peeled and cut into ½-inch pieces

¼ teaspoon table salt, plus salt for cooking potatoes

¼ cup extra-virgin olive oil

8 ounces plant-based ground meat

1 recipe Mexican Chorizo Seasoning (page 11)

3 tablespoons cider vinegar

12 (6-inch) corn tortillas, warmed

Finely chopped white onion

Fresh cilantro leaves

Lime wedges

why this recipe works The traditional Mexican taco filling pairing chorizo with potatoes is as ingenious as it is delicious. When fried, Mexican chorizo falls into crumbles, producing fragrant red juices that bathe everything around it in spice, fat, and vinegar. Potatoes pair so well because they readily absorb the luscious drippings, dispersing and diffusing the flavor so the overall effect is pleasingly piquant rather than overpoweringly spicy. To accomplish this feat with plant-based meat, we use a homemade spice blend to mimic the spicy-sweet flavor of Mexican chorizo. Adding some cider vinegar amplifies the flavors and provides the sausage's signature tang, and adding extra oil with the mashed potatoes gives us the lush richness that's essential for chorizo. A bright yet creamy green salsa of tomatillos, avocado, cilantro, and jalapeños lightens and balances the hearty filling. Chopped white onion provides a nice sharp crunch that complements the soft, rich taco filling, so we don't recommend omitting it. For a spicier salsa, use two jalapeños.

1 for the salsa verde: Process all ingredients in food processor until smooth, about 1 minute, scraping down sides of bowl as needed. Transfer to bowl and season with salt and pepper to taste. (Sauce can be refrigerated for up to 3 days; let come to room temperature before serving.)

2 for the filling: Bring 1 quart water to boil in 12-inch nonstick skillet over high heat. Add potatoes and 1 teaspoon salt. Reduce heat to medium, cover, and cook until potatoes are fully tender, about 8 minutes. Drain potatoes and transfer to medium bowl. Using potato masher, mash half of potatoes.

3 Wipe skillet clean with paper towels. Heat oil in now-empty skillet over medium heat until shimmering. Add ground meat and cook, breaking up meat into rough ½-inch pieces with wooden spoon, until firm pieces form, about 3 minutes. Stir in chorizo seasoning and ¼ teaspoon salt and cook until fragrant, about 30 seconds.

4 Off heat, stir in vinegar and let sit until steam subsides and skillet cools slightly, about 5 minutes. Fold potatoes into meat mixture until evenly distributed. Divide filling evenly among tortillas and serve, passing sauce, onion, cilantro, and lime wedges separately.

chorizo, corn, and tomato tostadas with lime crema

serves 4 to 6

total time 40 minutes

1 (14-ounce) bag green coleslaw mix

1 tablespoon minced jarred jalapeños, plus ¼ cup brine, divided

¾ teaspoon plus ⅛ teaspoon table salt, divided

½ cup plant-based or dairy sour cream

3 tablespoons lime juice (2 limes), divided

2 tablespoons extra-virgin olive oil

8 ounces plant-based ground meat

1 recipe Mexican Chorizo Seasoning (page 11)

3 cups frozen corn, thawed

3 tablespoons cider vinegar

6 ounces cherry tomatoes, quartered

1 (15-ounce) can black beans, rinsed

¼ cup vegetable broth

12 (6-inch) corn tostadas

why this recipe works Flat, crisped corn tortillas that serve as a crunchy base for a pile of flavorful toppings are a popular Mexican street food often eaten as a snack. Our meal-size version is mounded with highly seasoned plant-based meat, mashed black beans, corn, cherry tomatoes, crisp cabbage, and a lime-spiked crema. The meaty filling involves sautéing plant-based ground meat with our homemade chorizo seasoning blend. Corn adds pops of contrasting sweetness—we use frozen for year-round convenience. While the chorizo and corn cook, we spread our tostada shells with a mixture of mashed black beans and pickled jalapeño and warm them in the oven. We also put some of the jalapeño brine to work to quick-pickle the cabbage topping (using store-bought coleslaw mix instead of chopping up a head of cabbage is a timesaver). To amp up the richness factor, we mix up a tangy crema of sour cream and lime juice to spoon over the assembled tostadas. Look for tostadas next to the taco kits at most supermarkets.

1 Adjust oven racks to upper-middle and lower-middle positions and heat oven to 450 degrees. Combine coleslaw, 3 tablespoons jalapeño brine, and ¼ teaspoon salt in bowl. Combine sour cream, 2 tablespoons lime juice, and ⅛ teaspoon salt in second bowl; set aside slaw and crema.

2 Heat oil in 12-inch nonstick skillet over medium heat until shimmering. Add ground meat, chorizo seasoning, and ¼ teaspoon salt and cook, breaking up meat with wooden spoon, until firm crumbles form, about 3 minutes. Stir in corn and cook until heated through, about 1 minute.

3 Off heat, stir in vinegar and let sit until steam subsides and skillet cools slightly, about 5 minutes. Fold in tomatoes and remaining 1 tablespoon lime juice.

4 Microwave beans, broth, jalapeños and remaining 1 tablespoon brine, and remaining ¼ teaspoon salt in bowl until hot, about 2 minutes. Mash beans with potato masher until spreadable, then spread evenly over tostadas. Divide tostadas between 2 rimmed baking sheets and bake until heated through, about 5 minutes. Divide meat mixture among tostadas, then top with slaw and crema. Serve.

meat-and-bean burritos

serves 4
total time 35 minutes

1 tablespoon vegetable oil

1 onion, chopped fine

½ teaspoon table salt

1 tablespoon ground cumin

1 teaspoon chipotle chile powder

12 ounces plant-based ground meat

1 (15-ounce) can pinto beans, rinsed

½ cup water

4 (10-inch) flour tortillas

4 ounces plant-based or dairy cheddar cheese, shredded (1 cup)

2 cups shredded iceberg lettuce

1 avocado, halved, pitted, and cut into ½-inch pieces

1 tomato, cored and cut into ½-inch pieces

why this recipe works A Tex Mex–style meat-and-bean burrito may just be the ultimate busy-day meal: Not only is it superquick to make, but you can pick it up and take it with you if you've got too much going on to sit down for lunch or dinner. A bean-and-bean burrito, as anyone who's tried one while looking to cut down on or eliminate their meat intake will agree, just isn't the same. Plant-based meat to the rescue! Subbing it in for beef here means that these burritos pack all the meaty goodness you crave from a burrito. First, we soften an onion and bloom a few teaspoons of cumin and chile powder in oil, and then we add the plant-based meat, breaking it up into juicy, substantial crumbles. Pinto beans go in next; we give half of them a mash to make the filling more cohesive. After adding a few well-chosen accompaniments (you can't go wrong with cheese, lettuce, avocado, and tomato), we're ready to roll. And if you are sitting down for this feast, go all out and serve with sour cream, salsa, guacamole, and a side of Mexican or white rice, if desired.

1 Heat oil in 12-inch nonstick skillet over medium heat until shimmering. Add onion and salt and cook until softened and lightly browned, 5 to 7 minutes. Stir in cumin and chile powder and cook until fragrant, about 30 seconds. Add ground meat and cook, breaking up meat with wooden spoon, until firm crumbles form, about 3 minutes. Stir in beans and water and cook, mashing half of beans with back of spoon, until mixture is heated through and thickened, 3 to 5 minutes.

2 Wrap tortillas in damp dish towel and microwave until warm and pliable, about 1 minute. Arrange tortillas on counter. Divide meat-and-bean filling, cheese, lettuce, avocado, and tomato evenly across bottom third of tortillas, leaving 1-inch border. Working with 1 burrito at a time, fold sides of tortilla over filling, then fold up bottom of tortilla and roll tightly around filling. Serve.

empanadas with olives and raisins

serves 4
total time 1½ hours

1 tablespoon vegetable oil

1 onion, chopped fine

2 jalapeño chiles, stemmed, seeded, and minced

¼ teaspoon table salt

12 ounces plant-based ground meat

1 teaspoon ground cumin

¼ teaspoon pepper

¼ cup minced fresh cilantro

¼ cup pitted green olives, chopped

¼ cup raisins

1 recipe Plant-Based Pie Dough (page 13)

why this recipe works Handheld foods are more fun to eat, period. These empanadas are no exception. Sturdy pastries that can be stuffed with anything from meat to veggies to fruit, empanadas are popular throughout Latin America. Of special interest to us were the ground beef–filled empanadas common in Argentina, to which we give a plant-based twist. First, we pan sear plant-based meat with an onion and a couple minced jalapeños, stirring and breaking up the meat regularly to achieve a crumbly texture. Cumin, raisins, and chopped olives bring Argentinian flair to the filling. Once the dough (which comes together quickly in a food processor) is securely crimped around the filling, the pies are ready for baking. The hardest part of the whole process is the last step: waiting for the pies to cool before grabbing one and digging in. We prefer to make our own crust here, but you can substitute two 9-inch store-bought plant-based or dairy-based pie dough rounds, if desired.

1 Heat oil in 12-inch nonstick skillet over medium heat until shimmering. Add onion, jalapeños, and salt and cook until softened, about 5 minutes. Add ground meat and cook, breaking up meat with wooden spoon, until firm crumbles form, 2 to 3 minutes. Stir in cumin and pepper and cook until fragrant, about 30 seconds. Transfer filling to bowl and let cool completely. Stir in cilantro, olives, and raisins. (Filling can be refrigerated for up to 24 hours.)

2 Adjust oven rack to upper-middle position and heat oven to 375 degrees. Line rimmed baking sheet with parchment paper. Working with 1 dough disk at a time, sprinkle dough with flour and roll between 2 large sheets of parchment paper into 9-inch circle. (If dough cracks while rolling, allow it to soften further at room temperature, then pinch cracks closed and continue rolling. If dough becomes too soft, refrigerate briefly until chilled and set.) Remove parchment on top of dough.

3 Cut dough rounds in half. Arrange one-quarter of filling on 1 side of each dough half, leaving ½-inch border. Lightly brush edges of dough with water and fold dough over filling, pressing along sides to adhere. Crimp edges with floured tines of fork to seal, then transfer hand pies to prepared sheet.

4 Bake until pies have puffed and exteriors have lightly browned, about 35 minutes. Transfer hand pies to wire rack and let cool for 10 minutes before serving.

chapter 3
pasta, noodles, and bowls

big-batch weeknight meat sauce

makes about 6 cups; enough for 2 pounds of pasta
total time 50 minutes

4 ounces white mushrooms, trimmed and quartered

1 onion, chopped coarse

1 tablespoon extra-virgin olive oil

½ teaspoon table salt

½ teaspoon pepper

6 garlic cloves, minced

1 tablespoon tomato paste

1 tablespoon minced fresh oregano, divided, or 1 teaspoon dried

¼ teaspoon red pepper flakes

1 (14.5-ounce) can diced tomatoes, drained with ¼ cup juice reserved

12 ounces plant-based ground meat

1 (28-ounce) can crushed tomatoes

why this recipe works When it comes to Italian pasta, it doesn't matter whether you're Team Red Sauce or Team Meat Sauce. This weeknight-friendly, crowd-feeding recipe delivers the best of both worlds, so you don't have to choose. The sauce is garlicky and sweetly tomatoey thanks to a trifecta of tomatoes—crushed, diced, and paste—for ideal chunky-smooth texture and deep flavor. It's also eminently satiating thanks to the inclusion of both crumbled plant-based meat and mushrooms. We first develop a fond by searing mushrooms and an onion (finely chopped to help them integrate into the sauce), holding the meat back until later to ensure that it stays succulent and juicy. We then deglaze the pan with a splash of the juice from the canned tomatoes, scraping all that flavorful browning back into the sauce. The sauce takes just 45 minutes and can be prepared up to a month in advance, so you can use half a batch of this generously portioned sauce for dinner tonight and save the rest for whenever the next craving hits. If using dried oregano, add the entire amount with the garlic in step 3.

1 Pulse mushrooms and onion in food processor until finely chopped, about 8 pulses, scraping down sides of bowl as needed.

2 Heat oil in large saucepan over medium-high heat until shimmering. Add onion-mushroom mixture, salt, and pepper and cook, stirring occasionally, until liquid has evaporated, 4 to 6 minutes. Spread mixture into even layer in bottom of saucepan and continue to cook, stirring occasionally, until fond forms, 4 to 6 minutes.

3 Stir in garlic, tomato paste, 2 teaspoons oregano, and pepper flakes and cook until fragrant, about 30 seconds. Stir in reserved tomato juice, scraping up any browned bits. Add ground meat and cook, breaking up meat with wooden spoon, until firm crumbles form, about 3 minutes.

4 Stir in crushed and diced tomatoes and bring to simmer, then reduce heat to low and simmer, stirring occasionally, until sauce has thickened and tomatoes have broken down, 15 to 20 minutes. Stir in remaining 1 teaspoon oregano and season with salt and pepper to taste. (Sauce can be refrigerated for up to 3 days or frozen for up to 1 month.)

tagliatelle with weeknight bolognese

serves 4 to 6

total time 1 hour

1 onion, chopped coarse

1 large carrot, peeled and chopped coarse

1 celery rib, chopped coarse

2 tablespoons extra-virgin olive oil

½ teaspoon table salt, plus salt for cooking pasta

¼ teaspoon pepper

3 tablespoons tomato paste

½ cup dry red wine

12 ounces plant-based ground meat

2 cups vegetable broth

1 pound linguine or tagliatelle

Plant-based or dairy Parmesan cheese (optional)

why this recipe works Team Meat Sauce, this one's for you. An Italian bolognese is thick, rich, homey sustenance: the meatiest of sauces. There are many ways to make it, from long-cooked Sunday-supper versions featuring several different cuts of meat to quicker versions made with ground beef. This fast, no-compromise meatless version is every bit as comforting as a hug from an Italian grandmother. The only tomato in this dish comes from a few tablespoons of tomato paste, which boosts the sauce's umami flavor and deepens its color. Sautéing the mirepoix of onion, carrot, and celery yields plenty of flavorful fond, so there's no need to sear the plant-based meat here. Instead, we cook the meat gently for just a few minutes before adding our liquid. The sauce looks loose at first, but it thickens as the pasta soaks up the extra moisture. Tagliatelle is typically made with eggs; if that's a concern, look for egg-free tagliatelle or use another long, wide pasta such as linguine. You can use store-bought Parmesan or make our Plant-Based Parmesan (page 12), if desired.

1 Pulse onion, carrot, and celery in food processor until finely chopped and mixture has paste-like consistency, 12 to 15 pulses, scraping down sides of bowl as needed.

2 Heat oil in Dutch oven over medium-high heat until shimmering. Add vegetable mixture, salt, and pepper and cook, stirring occasionally, until liquid has evaporated, 6 to 8 minutes. Spread mixture into even layer in bottom of pot and continue to cook, stirring occasionally, until fond forms, 6 to 8 minutes. Stir in tomato paste and cook until paste is rust-colored and bottom of pot is dark brown, 1 to 2 minutes.

3 Stir in wine, scraping up any browned bits, and cook until nearly evaporated, 1 to 2 minutes. Reduce heat to medium, stir in ground meat, and cook until meat begins to clump, about 3 minutes. Stir in broth and bring to simmer. Cover, reduce heat to low, and simmer for 15 minutes (sauce will look thin). Remove from heat and season with salt and pepper to taste.

4 Meanwhile, bring 4 quarts water to boil in large pot. Add pasta and 1 tablespoon salt and cook, stirring often, until al dente. Reserve ½ cup cooking water, then drain pasta and add it to pot with sauce, tossing to combine. Adjust consistency with reserved cooking water as needed and season with salt and pepper to taste. Serve with Parmesan, if using.

spaghetti with sausage and spring vegetables

serves 6
total time 1 hour

6 ounces cherry tomatoes, halved

3 tablespoons extra-virgin olive oil, divided, plus extra for drizzling

½ teaspoon table salt, divided, plus salt for cooking pasta

¼ teaspoon pepper

1 pound spaghetti

12 ounces plant-based ground meat

1 recipe Sweet Italian Sausage Seasoning (page 11)

3 garlic cloves, minced

12 ounces zucchini, halved lengthwise and sliced ¼ inch thick

1 pound asparagus, trimmed and cut on bias into 1-inch lengths

1 cup frozen peas, thawed

¼ cup minced fresh chives and/or mint, divided

¼ cup plant-based or dairy Parmesan cheese or dairy Pecorino Romano cheese, plus extra for serving (optional)

why this recipe works Sausage and green vegetables are classic Italian pasta add-ins, and this dish celebrates both in equal measure. To make sure that the plant-based sausage holds its own amid the 2-plus pounds of spring produce in this recipe, we load it up with lots of fresh garlic and a generous sprinkle of our homemade Italian sausage seasoning (a mixture of fennel seeds, thyme, and garlic powder). Every pasta dish needs a great sauce, and this one comes from an unusual suspect: zucchini. Intentionally overcooking the zucchini until it starts to break down in the pan creates the base for a silky, light, clingy sauce into which we stir asparagus and peas. A handful of ruby-red marinated cherry tomatoes and a scattering of herbs provide a final flourish, and to tie it all together, we add a little Parmesan. (Pecorino Romano is great here, too.) You can use store-bought Parmesan or make our Plant-Based Parmesan (page 12), if desired.

1 Toss tomatoes, 1 tablespoon oil, ¼ teaspoon salt, and pepper together in bowl; set aside. Bring 4 quarts water to boil in large pot. Add pasta and 1 tablespoon salt and cook, stirring often, until al dente. Reserve ½ cup cooking water, then drain pasta and return it to pot.

2 Meanwhile, heat 1 tablespoon oil in 12-inch nonstick skillet over medium heat until shimmering. Add ground meat and cook, breaking up meat with wooden spoon, until firm crumbles form, about 3 minutes. Stir in Italian sausage seasoning and garlic and cook until fragrant, about 30 seconds; transfer to bowl.

3 Heat remaining 1 tablespoon oil in now-empty skillet over medium-low heat until shimmering. Add zucchini and remaining ¼ teaspoon salt and cook, covered, until softened and beginning to break down, 8 to 10 minutes. Stir in asparagus, peas, and ½ cup water and bring to simmer over medium-high heat. Cover and cook until asparagus is crisp-tender, about 2 minutes.

4 Add meat mixture, vegetable mixture with its liquid, and 3 tablespoons chives to pasta and toss to combine. Adjust consistency with reserved cooking water as needed and season with salt and pepper to taste. Transfer to serving bowl; spoon tomatoes and their juices over top; and sprinkle with Parmesan, if using, and remaining 1 tablespoon chives. Drizzle with extra oil and sprinkle with extra Parmesan, if using. Serve.

orecchiette with broccoli rabe and sausage

serves 4 to 6
total time 40 minutes

- 1 tablespoon extra-virgin olive oil, plus extra for drizzling
- 12 ounces plant-based ground meat
- 6 garlic cloves, minced
- 1 recipe Sweet Italian Sausage Seasoning (page 11)
- 1 pound broccoli rabe, trimmed and cut into 1½-inch pieces

  Table salt for cooking broccoli rabe and pasta
- 1 pound orecchiette
- ¼ cup plant-based or dairy Parmesan cheese or dairy Pecorino Romano cheese, plus extra for serving (optional)

why this recipe works Orecchiette (meaning "little ears" in Italian) is a small, bowl-shaped pasta that's perfect for cradling thick sauces and chunky ingredients like the broccoli rabe and plant-based Italian sausage in this hearty preparation based on an iconic southern Italian dish. This pasta dish is also extremely efficient to make. We boil the broccoli rabe just until crisp-tender to temper the assertive green, and then we use that same cooking water to boil the pasta—traditional and convenient! The aromatic fennel, thyme, and garlic mingle beautifully with the greens' vegetal bitterness. As we do in Spaghetti with Sausage and Spring Vegetables (page 88), we give plant-based meat a sausagey flavor profile by mixing it with our homemade Italian sausage seasoning. This allows us to tailor its flavors to our exact liking rather than relying on preseasoned store-bought sausages. You can use store-bought Parmesan or make our Plant-Based Parmesan (page 12), if desired.

1 Heat oil in 12-inch nonstick skillet over medium heat until shimmering. Add ground meat and cook, breaking up meat with wooden spoon, until firm crumbles form, about 3 minutes. Stir in garlic and Italian sausage seasoning and cook until fragrant, about 30 seconds; remove from heat.

2 Meanwhile, bring 4 quarts water to boil in large pot. Add broccoli rabe and 1 tablespoon salt and cook, stirring often, until crisp-tender, about 2 minutes. Using slotted spoon, transfer broccoli rabe to skillet with meat mixture.

3 Return water to boil, add pasta, and cook, stirring often, until al dente. Reserve 1 cup cooking water, then drain pasta and return it to pot. Add meat–broccoli rabe mixture; Parmesan, if using; and ⅓ cup reserved cooking water and toss to combine. Adjust consistency with remaining ⅔ cup reserved cooking water as needed and season with salt and pepper to taste. Drizzle with extra oil and sprinkle with extra Parmesan, if using. Serve.

meatballs and marinara

serves 4 to 6

total time 1½ hours

sauce

- 2 tablespoons extra-virgin olive oil
- 1 onion, chopped fine
- 2 garlic cloves, minced
- 1 teaspoon dried oregano
- ⅛ teaspoon red pepper flakes
- 2 tablespoons tomato paste
- ¼ cup dry red wine
- 1 (28-ounce) can crushed tomatoes
- ¼ cup water
- 2 tablespoons chopped fresh basil

meatballs and pasta

- ½ cup panko bread crumbs
- 2 tablespoons water
- ½ teaspoon garlic powder
- ½ teaspoon dried oregano
- ¼ teaspoon table salt, plus salt for cooking pasta
- ⅛ teaspoon pepper
- 12 ounces plant-based ground meat
- 1 pound spaghetti
- Plant-based or dairy Parmesan cheese (optional)

why this recipe works Meatballs and marinara sauce is an iconic dish that's also super family-friendly, so a plant-based version had better be top-notch to please everybody, with tender, moist meatballs and the brightest, freshest-tasting tomato sauce. These plant-based meatballs mimic the springy-tender texture of classic meatballs so well you'd never know they're meat-free. We skip the usual messy pan searing, dropping the meatballs right into the simmering sauce to cook through. As for the flavors, we keep them simple and classic. Garlic powder is milder and nuttier-tasting than fresh garlic, and together with dried oregano, it gives the meatballs big flavor while keeping prep work minimal. A panko panade both binds the meat and keeps it tender. Concentrated, umami-packed tomato paste and red wine add depth to our sauce. You can use store-bought Parmesan or make our Plant-Based Parmesan (page 12), if desired. This recipe can be easily doubled.

1 for the sauce: Heat oil in Dutch oven over medium heat until shimmering. Add onion and cook until softened, about 5 minutes. Stir in garlic, oregano, and pepper flakes and cook until fragrant, about 30 seconds.

2. Stir in tomato paste and cook until fragrant, about 1 minute. Stir in wine and cook until slightly thickened, about 2 minutes. Stir in tomatoes and water and bring to simmer, then reduce heat to low and simmer gently until flavors meld, about 30 minutes. Stir in basil and season with salt and pepper to taste.

3 for the meatballs and pasta: While sauce simmers, stir panko, water, garlic powder, oregano, salt, and pepper in large bowl until evenly combined. Break ground meat into small pieces and add to bowl with panko mixture. Gently knead with your hands until mixture is well combined. Using your moistened hands, pinch off and roll meat mixture into 1½-inch meatballs. (You should have 12 meatballs.) Transfer meatballs to plate and refrigerate for at least 15 minutes or up to 24 hours.

4 Nestle meatballs into sauce and return to simmer over medium-high heat. Cover, reduce heat to medium-low, and simmer until meatballs are firm and warmed through, about 15 minutes. Season with salt and pepper to taste.

5 Bring 4 quarts water to boil in large pot. Add pasta and 1 tablespoon salt and cook, stirring often, until al dente. Reserve ½ cup cooking water, then drain pasta and return it to pot. Add several spoonfuls of sauce (without meatballs) to pasta and toss to combine. Add reserved cooking water as needed to adjust consistency and season with salt and pepper to taste. Serve pasta with meatballs; Parmesan, if using; and remaining sauce.

pasta with sausage, mushrooms, and peas

serves 4
total time 1 hour

2   tablespoons extra-virgin olive oil, divided

12 ounces plant-based ground meat

1½ tablespoons Sweet Italian Sausage Seasoning (page 11)

1   pound cremini mushrooms, trimmed and sliced thin

2   shallots, chopped

1   teaspoon pepper

¾   teaspoon table salt

¼   teaspoon red pepper flakes

½   cup dry white wine

4   cups water

12 ounces (4½ cups) medium pasta shells

2   cups frozen peas

1   cup chopped fresh basil

2   teaspoons grated lemon zest, plus lemon wedges for serving

    Plant-based or dairy Parmesan cheese (optional)

why this recipe works This one-pot pasta dinner upends the pasta playbook. Conventional wisdom calls for ridding the pasta of excess starch by boiling it in plenty of liquid that's later drained away. Here, though, we add just enough liquid to hydrate the pasta and simmer the pasta vigorously, intentionally releasing its starch to help the liquid thicken into a luxurious, clingy sauce. Bulked up with plant-based meat and mushrooms and enlivened with lemon zest, sweet peas, and fresh basil, this dish is the perfect remedy for the winter doldrums (but you can, and should, enjoy it any time of year). After seasoning and cooking the meat, we set it aside to prevent it from drying out while we sear the vegetables. Deglazing the pan with white wine adds welcome acidity and loosens the flavorful browned bits so we can scrape them up and mix them back into the sauce. You can substitute 12 ounces (3⅓ cups) orecchiette for the shells. You can use store-bought Parmesan or make our Plant-Based Parmesan (page 12), if desired.

1 Heat 1 tablespoon oil in Dutch oven over medium heat until shimmering. Add ground meat and cook, breaking up meat with wooden spoon, until firm crumbles form, about 3 minutes. Stir in Italian sausage seasoning and cook until fragrant, about 30 seconds; transfer to bowl.

2 Heat remaining 1 tablespoon oil in now-empty pot over high heat until shimmering. Add mushrooms, shallots, pepper, salt, and pepper flakes and cook, stirring occasionally, until liquid has evaporated and browned bits have formed on bottom of pot, about 15 minutes.

3 Stir in wine and cook, scraping up any browned bits, until liquid has evaporated, about 2 minutes. Stir in water and bring to boil. Stir in pasta, bring to vigorous simmer, and cook uncovered, stirring often, until pasta is tender, about 10 minutes (some liquid will remain in bottom of pot).

4 Off heat, add peas, basil, lemon zest, and meat mixture. Stir vigorously for 1 minute, until sauce has thickened slightly. Serve with lemon wedges and Parmesan, if using.

meaty skillet mac

serves 4
total time 45 minutes

1 tablespoon extra-virgin olive oil

1 onion, chopped fine

1 red bell pepper, stemmed, seeded, and chopped fine

½ teaspoon table salt

¼ teaspoon pepper

12 ounces plant-based ground meat

6 garlic cloves, minced

1½ teaspoons dried oregano

1 (29-ounce) can tomato sauce

2 cups vegetable broth

8 ounces (2 cups) elbow macaroni

4 ounces plant-based or dairy cheddar cheese, shredded (1 cup) (optional)

why this recipe works Even if you didn't grow up eating Hamburger Helper, there's something inherently nostalgic about a big bowlful of saucy, ground-beefy pasta. Major bonuses to our plant-based recipe: It takes just one pan and comes together in 45 minutes, no flavor packets required. We start by sautéing onion and bell pepper to build a flavorful backbone for the meaty sauce, adding the plant-based meat and stirring to break up clumps once the aromatics are softened. (This vegetable-first approach works best with plant-based meat since the meat cooks so quickly that it can overcook if added before the aromatics.) Bright store-bought tomato sauce is a big time saver; we loosen its consistency with vegetable broth and then stir in a couple cups of elbow macaroni to cook right in the sauce. Once the sauce thickens and the pasta is perfectly al dente, it's time to grab a fork and sink into the pure, unfussy comfort.

1 Heat oil in 12-inch nonstick skillet over medium heat until shimmering. Add onion, bell pepper, salt, and pepper and cook until softened and beginning to brown, 5 to 7 minutes. Stir in ground meat and cook, breaking up meat with wooden spoon, until firm crumbles form, about 3 minutes. Stir in garlic and oregano and cook until fragrant, about 30 seconds.

2 Stir in tomato sauce, broth, and macaroni and bring to boil. Cover, reduce heat to low, and simmer, stirring occasionally, until macaroni is tender, 10 to 12 minutes. Remove from heat and let sit until sauce is thickened, about 5 minutes. Season with salt and pepper to taste. Sprinkle with cheddar, if using. Serve.

toasted orzo pilaf with meatballs, fennel, and orange

serves 4
total time 1¼ hours

½ cup panko bread crumbs

2 tablespoons water

1¼ teaspoons baharat, divided

¾ teaspoon table salt, divided

⅛ teaspoon pepper

12 ounces plant-based ground meat

2 tablespoons extra-virgin olive oil, divided

1 fennel bulb, ¼ cup fronds chopped, stalks discarded, bulb halved, cored, and chopped fine

2 garlic cloves, minced

Pinch red pepper flakes

1¼ cups orzo

2 cups vegetable broth

½ cup dry white wine

¼ cup pitted kalamata olives, chopped

¼ cup shelled pistachios, toasted and chopped

1 teaspoon grated orange zest, plus orange wedges for serving

why this recipe works Licoricey fresh fennel, fruity orange zest, and briny olives bring Mediterranean sunshine to this meatball pilaf. Adapting a favorite test kitchen recipe for Greek-inspired lamb meatballs and orzo, we replace the lamb with—you guessed it!—plant-based meat. It is milder in flavor than rich, grassy-tasting lamb; here that quality works to the pilaf's advantage, letting the delicate nuances of the fennel and orange zest come through. With the addition of the Middle Eastern spice blend baharat to the meatballs, the pilaf becomes a striking fusion of Greek and Middle Eastern flavors. Panko bread crumbs stirred into the mix act as a panade to keep the meat juicy. After quickly browning the meatballs, we nestle them in the simmering orzo to finish cooking. The crunch from chopped pistachios sprinkled over the pilaf is a welcome textural contrast. If baharat is unavailable, substitute a combination of ¾ teaspoon cumin, ¼ teaspoon pepper, ¼ teaspoon ground coriander, ⅛ teaspoon ground cinnamon, and ⅛ teaspoon ground cloves.

1 Stir panko, water, ¾ teaspoon baharat, ¼ teaspoon salt, and pepper in large bowl until evenly combined. Break ground meat into small pieces and add to bowl with panko mixture. Gently knead with your hands until mixture is well combined. Using your moistened hands, pinch off and roll meat mixture into 1½-inch meatballs. (You should have 12 meatballs.) Transfer meatballs to plate and refrigerate for at least 15 minutes or up to 24 hours.

2 Heat 1 tablespoon oil in 12-inch nonstick skillet over medium-high heat until shimmering. Add meatballs and cook until well browned all over, 2 to 3 minutes. Transfer meatballs to large plate.

3 Heat remaining 1 tablespoon oil in now-empty skillet over medium heat until shimmering. Add fennel bulb and remaining ½ teaspoon salt and cook until softened and lightly browned, 5 to 7 minutes. Stir in garlic, pepper flakes, and remaining ½ teaspoon baharat and cook until fragrant, about 30 seconds. Add orzo and cook, stirring frequently, until orzo is lightly browned, about 5 minutes.

4 Stir in broth and wine and bring to boil. Nestle meatballs into skillet and cook, stirring occasionally, until orzo is tender, about 10 minutes. Stir in olives, pistachios, and orange zest and season with salt and pepper to taste. Sprinkle with fennel fronds and serve with orange wedges.

one-pot stroganoff

serves 4

total time 45 minutes

2 tablespoons vegetable oil, divided

8 ounces white mushrooms, trimmed and sliced thin

½ teaspoon table salt, divided

1 onion, chopped fine

2 garlic cloves, minced

¾ teaspoon pepper, divided

12 ounces plant-based ground meat

3 tablespoons all-purpose flour

4 cups vegetable broth

¼ cup dry white wine

8 ounces (4 cups) wide egg-free noodles or egg noodles

½ cup plant-based or dairy sour cream, plus extra for serving

2 tablespoons minced fresh chives

why this recipe works In its classical form, stroganoff is a dish of sautéed beef (usually thinly sliced tenderloin or steak tips), mushrooms, and onion in a creamy sauce, typically served over egg noodles. It's simple and elegant and so, because you can never have too many one-pot pasta recipes in your back pocket, we created this fast, veg-friendly version using plant-based ground meat. We sauté thinly sliced white mushrooms to build up flavorful fond. Then, after softening onion and garlic, we add the meat and cook it just until it's crumbly and firm. To make our stroganoff a one-pot affair, we boil the noodles (egg noodles if you like to keep it traditional, or wide egg-free noodles for a vegan alternative) in the same pot. Cooking the noodles in vegetable broth and white wine instead of water makes for a superflavorful result once the liquid has reduced down into a glossy, luxurious sauce, thickened with flour and a dollop of sour cream for tang and creamy richness. You can substitute Greek yogurt for the sour cream, if desired.

1 Heat 1 tablespoon oil in Dutch oven over medium heat until shimmering. Add mushrooms and ¼ teaspoon salt and cook until liquid has evaporated and mushrooms begin to brown, 5 to 7 minutes; transfer to bowl.

2 Add remaining 1 tablespoon oil to now-empty pot and heat over medium heat until shimmering. Add onion, garlic, ½ teaspoon pepper, and ⅛ teaspoon salt and cook, stirring occasionally, until onion is softened, about 5 minutes. Add ground meat, remaining ⅛ teaspoon salt, and remaining ¼ teaspoon pepper and cook, breaking up meat with wooden spoon, until firm crumbles form, about 3 minutes.

3 Add flour, stir to coat meat, and cook for 1 minute. Stir in broth and wine and bring to simmer, scraping up any browned bits. Stir in noodles, reduce heat to medium-low, and simmer gently, uncovered, until noodles are tender, 10 to 12 minutes, stirring occasionally and scraping up any browned bits.

4 Off heat, stir in sour cream and mushrooms and season with salt and pepper to taste. Sprinkle with chives. Serve, passing extra sour cream separately.

dan dan mian

serves 4 to 6
total time 50 minutes

¼ cup Chinese sesame paste or tahini

¼ cup soy sauce, divided

2 tablespoons seasoned rice vinegar

5 teaspoons hoisin sauce, divided

1 tablespoon Asian chili-garlic sauce

2 teaspoons sugar

1 pound fresh Chinese wheat noodles

2 tablespoons toasted sesame oil

3 tablespoons vegetable oil, divided

12 ounces plant-based ground meat

1 tablespoon Shaoxing wine or dry sherry

6 scallions, white parts sliced thin, green parts sliced thin on bias

3 garlic cloves, minced

1 teaspoon red pepper flakes

½ teaspoon ground Sichuan peppercorns, plus extra for serving (optional)

why this recipe works Dan dan mian—Sichuan noodles awash in a moderately spicy chili sauce and heaped with savory bits of pork—gets a supersatisfying plant-based twist. Substantial and filling thanks to the meat and fresh wheat noodles, rich and spicy from toasted sesame oil and a pepper-spiked garlic oil, and with a bit of crunch from thinly sliced scallions, each bite contains a world of flavor. Plant-based meat, broken into small pieces and seared until lightly browned, stands in for the traditional pork. We whisk up a sauce of hoisin and chili-garlic sauce for sweet heat, glutamate-rich soy to underscore the meatiness, and a splash of rice vinegar for zing. Chinese sesame paste, made from toasted sesame seeds, thickens the sauce and bolsters its sesame flavor; tahini is a good substitute in a pinch. We prefer the chewy texture of fresh, eggless Chinese wheat noodles here. If they aren't available and you include eggs in your diet, substitute fresh lo mein or ramen noodles or 8 ounces of dried lo mein noodles.

1 Whisk 1 cup hot water, sesame paste, 3 tablespoons soy sauce, vinegar, 2 teaspoons hoisin, chili-garlic sauce, and sugar together in bowl; set aside.

2 Bring 4 quarts water to boil in large pot. Add noodles and cook, stirring often, until almost tender (center should still be firm with slightly opaque dot). Drain noodles. Rinse under hot running water, tossing with tongs, for 1 minute. Drain well and return to pot. Add sesame oil and toss to coat; cover to keep warm.

3 Heat 1 tablespoon vegetable oil in 12-inch nonstick skillet over medium-high heat until shimmering. Add ground meat and cook, breaking up meat with wooden spoon, until firm crumbles form, about 3 minutes. Stir in Shaoxing wine, remaining 1 tablespoon soy sauce, and remaining 1 tablespoon hoisin and cook until all liquid has evaporated, 1 to 3 minutes. Transfer meat mixture to pot with noodles.

4 Add remaining 2 tablespoons vegetable oil; scallion whites; garlic; pepper flakes; and peppercorns, if using, to now-empty skillet and cook over medium heat until fragrant, about 2 minutes. Add to pot with noodles along with reserved tahini mixture and toss to coat. Sprinkle with scallion greens and extra peppercorns, if using. Adjust consistency with hot water as needed. Serve.

savory soba noodles with eggplant and miso

serves 4
total time 50 minutes

3 tablespoons white miso

3 tablespoons extra-virgin olive oil, divided

4 scallions (2 minced; 2 sliced thin on bias, green and white parts separated)

⅛ teaspoon pepper

12 ounces soba noodles

1 pound eggplant, cut into ½-inch pieces

12 ounces plant-based ground meat

2 teaspoons soy sauce

2 garlic cloves, minced

1 teaspoon grated fresh ginger

1 teaspoon toasted sesame oil

why this recipe works Miso, a Japanese paste made from fermented soybeans, is a total umami bomb. Here, as the base of an earthy, salty sauce, its nuanced savoriness amps up the flavor of the plant-based meat in these irresistible noodles. The silky sauce clings to the warm, slightly chewy soba noodles as well as to the golden-brown cubes of sautéed eggplant and, of course, the meat, which we crumble into bits as it cooks so its presence is evident in every bite. We sear the eggplant until its exterior is browned and crispy, its interior meltingly creamy. We then season the meat with soy sauce (another source of umami), ginger, garlic, and toasted sesame oil for its inimitable nuttiness. The marriage of the potent miso sauce–coated noodles, caramelized eggplant, and seasoned meat makes for a dinner that's layered with flavor but quick and easy enough for any night of the week.

1 Whisk miso, 2 tablespoons olive oil, minced scallions, and pepper together in medium bowl. Bring 4 quarts water to boil in large pot. Add noodles and cook, stirring often, until tender. Reserve ½ cup cooking water, then drain noodles and return them to pot. Add all but 2 teaspoons miso mixture, tossing to coat, then adjust consistency with reserved cooking water as needed. Season with salt and pepper to taste, cover to keep warm, and set aside until ready to serve.

2 Heat 2 teaspoons olive oil in 12-inch nonstick skillet over medium-high heat until shimmering. Add eggplant and cook, stirring occasionally, until tender and deeply browned, 8 to 10 minutes. Combine eggplant and remaining 2 teaspoons miso mixture in bowl, tossing to coat; cover with aluminum foil and set aside until ready to serve.

3 Heat remaining 1 teaspoon olive oil in now-empty skillet over medium-high heat until shimmering. Add ground meat and cook, breaking up meat with wooden spoon, until firm crumbles form, about 3 minutes. Add soy sauce, garlic, ginger, sesame oil, and sliced scallion whites and cook until fragrant, about 30 seconds; remove from heat.

4 Divide noodles among individual serving bowls. Top with eggplant and meat mixture and sprinkle with remaining sliced scallion greens. Serve.

lion's head meatballs with cabbage and rice noodles

serves 4 to 6
total time 1¼ hours

1½ pounds plant-based ground meat

2 scallions, white parts minced, green parts sliced thin

2 tablespoons soy sauce

2 tablespoons Shaoxing wine or dry sherry

4 teaspoons sugar

2 teaspoons grated fresh ginger

½ teaspoon table salt

½ teaspoon white pepper

4 cups vegetable broth

1 small head napa cabbage (1½ pounds), quartered lengthwise, cored, and cut crosswise into 2-inch pieces

4 ounces rice vermicelli

why this recipe works The evocative name of these giant meatballs hailing from eastern China refers to how the napa cabbage pieces they're served with fringe the spheres, evoking a lion's mane. We first fell in love with these lion's head meatballs when developing a recipe using traditional pork; in this adaptation, we do away with the animal protein but keep all the nuanced flavor. In our pork-based recipe, the meat is kneaded until its sticky proteins cross-link and bind to yield springy-textured meatballs. Since plant-based meat lacks the myosin responsible for this change in texture, here we save some time and skip the kneading. These meatballs are a bit more tender than the traditional pork version, but we still appreciate their flavor thanks to the scallions, soy sauce, Shaoxing wine, sugar, salt, fresh ginger, and white pepper we mix right in. To cook the meatballs, we gently braise them with the cabbage in vegetable broth while the rice noodles soften in a separate pot. The result: fittingly regal crowns to these slurpable noodle bowls. Depending on the brand of plant-based meat you use, these large meatballs may be slightly pink in the center when fully cooked. For the best results, make sure to shake all excess water from the noodles after rinsing them.

1 Combine ground meat, scallion whites, soy sauce, Shaoxing wine, sugar, ginger, salt, and white pepper in large bowl and gently knead with your hands until mixture is well combined. Using your moistened hands, pinch off and roll meat mixture into 2½-inch meatballs (you should have 8 meatballs). Transfer meatballs to plate and refrigerate for at least 30 minutes or up to 24 hours.

2 Bring broth to boil in Dutch oven over high heat. Add cabbage, reduce heat to low, cover, and simmer for 10 minutes. Arrange meatballs in pot (seven around perimeter and one in center; meatballs will not be totally submerged). Cover pot and continue to simmer until meatballs are firm and cabbage is tender, 20 to 25 minutes longer, turning meatballs to submerge exposed side halfway through simmering.

3 While cabbage and meatballs cook, bring 4 quarts water to boil in large pot. Off heat, add noodles and let sit until tender, about 10 minutes. Drain and rinse well under cold water, then distribute evenly among individual serving bowls. Ladle meatballs, cabbage, and broth over noodles in bowls. Sprinkle with scallion greens and serve.

bun cha

serves 4
total time 1 hour

noodles and salad

8 ounces rice vermicelli

1 head Boston lettuce
(8 ounces), leaves separated
and torn into bite-size pieces

1 English cucumber, quartered
lengthwise and sliced thin
on bias

1 cup fresh cilantro leaves
and stems, trimmed

1 cup fresh mint leaves,
torn if large

sauce

½–1 small Thai chile, stemmed
and minced

3 tablespoons sugar, divided

1 garlic clove, minced

⅔ cup hot water

5 tablespoons soy sauce

¼ cup lime juice (2 limes)

patties

1 large shallot, minced

12 ounces plant-based
ground meat

2 teaspoons vegetable oil

why this recipe works Vietnamese bun cha is a vibrant amalgam of pork, crisp lettuce and cucumber, bright herbs, and rice vermicelli, all united by a potent sweet-sour-salty sauce known as nuoc cham. The traditional version features grilled pork patties shaped like squished meatballs. Here, we swap the grill for a nonstick skillet and press the patties into ½-inch-thick disks to give them even more flat, brownable surface area than the originals. Nuoc cham traditionally includes fish sauce; to make up for its absence here, we substitute similarly salty soy sauce. We use the sauce two ways: A couple tablespoons go into the meat mixture, and the rest goes on the side for drizzling over the salad, meat, and noodles according to individual preference. For the best results, make sure to shake all excess water from the noodles after rinsing them. For a less spicy sauce, use only half the Thai chile. To serve, place platters of noodles, salad, sauce, and pork patties on the table and allow diners to assemble components to their taste.

1 for the noodles and salad: Bring 4 quarts water to boil in large pot. Off heat, add noodles and let sit until tender, about 10 minutes. Drain and rinse well under cold water, spread on large plate, and let sit at room temperature to dry. Arrange lettuce, cucumber, cilantro, and mint on large platter and refrigerate until ready to serve.

2 for the sauce: Using mortar and pestle (or on cutting board using flat side of chef's knife), mash Thai chile, 1 tablespoon sugar, and garlic to fine paste. Transfer to medium bowl and add hot water and remaining 2 tablespoons sugar. Stir until sugar is dissolved. Stir in soy sauce and lime juice; set aside.

3 for the patties: Combine shallot and 2 tablespoons reserved sauce in medium bowl. Break ground meat into small pieces and add to bowl with shallot mixture. Gently knead with your hands until mixture is well combined. Using your moistened hands, divide meat mixture into 12 lightly packed balls, then flatten into ½-inch-thick patties. Transfer patties to plate and refrigerate for at least 15 minutes or up to 24 hours.

4 Heat oil in 12-inch nonstick skillet over medium-high heat until just smoking. Using spatula, transfer patties to skillet and cook until well browned on first side, about 3 minutes. Flip patties and continue to cook until browned on second side and meat registers 130 to 135 degrees, about 2 minutes. Transfer patties to serving plate. Serve noodles, salad, sauce, and meat patties separately.

rice noodle bowl with scallion-meat patties and cucumber

serves 4

total time 1 hour

8 ounces rice vermicelli

5 tablespoons soy sauce

3 tablespoons plus 1 teaspoon toasted sesame oil, divided

1½ tablespoons grated fresh ginger

3 garlic cloves, minced

1 English cucumber, cut into 2-inch-long matchsticks

2 tablespoons seasoned rice vinegar

1 scallion, sliced thin on bias

12 ounces plant-based ground meat

¼ cup fresh cilantro leaves

why this recipe works Rice noodles, seasoned meat, and fresh veg make a charming three-part harmony in this easy bowl. As in our Bun Cha (page 108), we shape the plant-based meat into thin patties to help it get beautifully brown all over. We mix a single thinly sliced scallion into the meat before cooking the patties over medium-high heat, yielding nicely charred patties permeated with mild oniony flavor and crunchy scallion bits. The potent sauce of toasted sesame oil, soy sauce, fresh ginger, and garlic is incorporated two ways: Some we mix into the meat and the rest we toss with the rice noodles. Cilantro and long matchsticks of cooling quick-pickled cucumber provide a fresh finish. For the best results, make sure to shake all excess water from the noodles after rinsing them.

1 Bring 4 quarts water to boil in large pot. Off heat, add noodles and let sit until tender, about 10 minutes. Drain and rinse well under cold water; set aside. Whisk soy sauce, 2 tablespoons oil, ginger, and garlic together in large bowl. Combine cucumber and vinegar in second bowl.

2 Spray aluminum foil–lined rimmed baking sheet with vegetable oil spray. Combine scallion and 2 tablespoons soy sauce mixture in medium bowl. Break ground meat into small pieces and add to bowl with scallion mixture. Gently knead with your hands until mixture is well combined. Using your moistened hands, divide meat mixture into 12 lightly packed balls, then flatten into ½-inch-thick patties. Transfer patties to plate and refrigerate for at least 15 minutes or up to 24 hours.

3 Heat 2 teaspoons oil in 12-inch nonstick skillet over medium-high heat until just smoking. Using spatula, transfer 6 patties to skillet and cook until well browned on first side, about 3 minutes. Flip patties and continue to cook until browned on second side and meat registers 130 to 135 degrees, about 2 minutes. Transfer patties to plate and tent with aluminum foil while cooking remaining patties. Repeat with remaining 2 teaspoons oil and remaining 6 patties. Transfer patties to cutting board and chop into large pieces.

4 Add noodles to remaining soy sauce mixture and toss to combine. Divide noodles evenly among 4 bowls and top with meat, cucumber, and cilantro. Serve.

meaty zoodle bowl with mango and garam masala

serves 4
total time 30 minutes

- 1 large mango, peeled, pitted, and cut into ¼-inch pieces
- ¼ cup chopped fresh cilantro, divided
- 1 teaspoon grated lemon zest plus 3 tablespoons juice, divided
- ¾ cup plain plant-based yogurt or whole-milk dairy yogurt
- 3 garlic cloves, minced, divided
- 1 tablespoon plus 2 teaspoons vegetable oil, divided
- 12 ounces plant-based ground meat
- 2 teaspoons grated fresh ginger
- 4 teaspoons garam masala, divided
- ½ teaspoon table salt, divided
- ½ teaspoon pepper, divided
- 1½ pounds zucchini noodles, cut into 6-inch lengths, divided

why this recipe works Zucchini noodles are a lighter, fresher alternative to wheat-based or rice-based noodles, and when paired with warmly spiced meat and a cooling yogurt sauce, they're cause for real mealtime excitement. For big impact with little effort, we season plant-based meat with garam masala, an Indian spice blend containing an array of spices including cumin, coriander, cinnamon, and pepper. Fresh ginger and garlic bring their distinct bite to the mix; we give the meat a few minutes' head start before adding them and the garam masala to the skillet to prevent the spices from burning or mellowing too much in the heat. Chopped mango adds brilliant color and nectary sweetness. Two pounds of zucchini will yield 24 ounces of noodles; we prefer to make our own using a spiralizer, but in a pinch you can use store-bought.

1 Combine mango, 2 tablespoons cilantro, and 1 tablespoon lemon juice in bowl; season with salt and pepper to taste and set aside until ready to serve. Whisk yogurt, one-third garlic, lemon zest and remaining 2 tablespoons juice, and remaining 2 tablespoons cilantro together in bowl; season with salt and pepper to taste and set aside until ready to serve.

2 Heat 1 tablespoon oil in 12-inch nonstick skillet over medium heat until shimmering. Add ground meat and cook, breaking up meat with wooden spoon so that pieces are no smaller than ¼ to ½ inch, until firm crumbles form, about 3 minutes. Add ginger, 2 teaspoons garam masala, ¼ teaspoon salt, ¼ teaspoon pepper, and remaining garlic and cook until fragrant, about 30 seconds. Transfer to bowl, cover with aluminum foil to keep warm, and set aside until ready to serve.

3 Heat 1 teaspoon oil in now-empty skillet over medium-high heat until shimmering. Add 1 teaspoon garam masala, ⅛ teaspoon salt, ⅛ teaspoon pepper, and half of zucchini noodles and cook, tossing frequently, until crisp-tender, about 1 minute. Transfer to 2 individual serving bowls and repeat with remaining 1 teaspoon oil, remaining 1 teaspoon garam masala, remaining ⅛ teaspoon salt, remaining ⅛ teaspoon pepper, and remaining zucchini noodles. Top zucchini noodles with reserved meat, reserved mango mixture, and reserved yogurt sauce. Serve.

spinach and snap pea salad bowl with herbed meat patties

serves 4
total time 55 minutes

creamy avocado dressing

- 1 ripe avocado, halved, pitted, and cut into ½-inch pieces
- 2 tablespoons extra-virgin olive oil
- 1 teaspoon grated lemon zest plus 3 tablespoons juice
- 1 garlic clove, minced
- ¾ teaspoon table salt
- ¼ teaspoon pepper

salad

- 1 tablespoon minced fresh dill
- 1 tablespoon minced fresh tarragon
- 1 tablespoon grated lemon zest
- ⅛ teaspoon table salt
- ⅛ teaspoon pepper
- 12 ounces plant-based ground meat
- 2 teaspoons vegetable oil
- 8 ounces (8 cups) baby spinach
- 2 scallions, sliced thin
- 8 ounces seedless grapes, halved (¾ cup)
- 4 ounces sugar snap peas, strings removed, halved
- 4 radishes, trimmed, halved, and sliced thin
- 2 ounces (1 cup) alfalfa sprouts

why this recipe works Here's a sunny salad bowl with undeniable California vibes thanks to the sweet-tart pops from a handful of halved grapes and the creamy, lemony-garlicky avocado dressing. Bursting with feel-good freshness from spinach, snap peas, peppery radishes, and a pile of dainty alfalfa sprouts, it'll brighten up even the dreariest of days. Crispy bits of plant-based meat anchor all that freshness and give the bowl some serious staying power. To maximize the meat's surface area for browning and yield the most satisfying crunch, we press the meat (mixed with fresh dill, tarragon, and lemon zest to enliven its flavor profile) into thin patties, cook them in smoking-hot oil, and then chop them into bite-size pieces to scatter over the salad. Drizzle on the dreamy avocado dressing, and you've got a meal that deserves acclaim from coast to coast.

1 for the creamy avocado dressing: Process all ingredients in food processor until smooth, about 30 seconds, scraping down sides of bowl as needed. Thin dressing with up to 2 tablespoons water as needed and season with salt and pepper to taste.

2 for the salad: Spray aluminum foil–lined rimmed baking sheet with vegetable oil spray. Stir dill, tarragon, lemon zest, salt, and pepper together in large bowl. Break ground meat into small pieces and add to bowl with herb mixture. Gently knead with your hands until mixture is well combined. Using your moistened hands, divide meat mixture into 12 lightly packed balls, then flatten into ½-inch-thick patties. Transfer patties to plate and refrigerate for at least 15 minutes or up to 24 hours.

3 Heat oil in 12-inch nonstick skillet over medium-high heat until just smoking. Using spatula, transfer patties to skillet and cook until well browned on first side, about 3 minutes. Flip patties and continue to cook until browned on second side and meat registers 130 to 135 degrees, about 2 minutes. Transfer patties to cutting board and chop patties into large pieces.

4 Toss spinach and scallions with half of dressing to coat, then season with salt and pepper to taste. Divide among individual serving bowls, then top with meat, grapes, snap peas, and radishes. Drizzle with remaining dressing and top with alfalfa sprouts. Serve.

taco salad bowl

serves 4 to 6

total time 35 minutes

taco meat

- 1 tablespoon vegetable oil
- 1 onion, chopped fine
- ¼ teaspoon table salt
- 12 ounces plant-based ground meat
- 4 teaspoons chili powder
- 2 garlic cloves, minced
- 1 (8-ounce) can tomato sauce
- ½ cup vegetable broth
- 2 teaspoons cider vinegar
- 1 teaspoon packed light brown sugar

salad

- 2 romaine lettuce hearts (12 ounces), cut into 1-inch pieces
- 1 (15-ounce) can black beans, rinsed
- 8 ounces cherry or grape tomatoes, quartered
- 2 scallions, sliced thin
- ½ cup fresh cilantro leaves, divided
- 2 tablespoons lime juice, plus lime wedges for serving
- 2 cups tortilla chips, broken into 1-inch pieces

why this recipe works While we love a good old-fashioned taco (see our recipes on pages 68–75 for proof), there's something to be said for shaking up the formula once in a while. A taco salad bowl is basically just a deconstructed taco—all the usual suspects are present, plus a bonus helping of crisp, refreshing lettuce. And because you're loading up a bowl rather than a tortilla, you can really pile on the toppings if that's your jam. Here we season the plant-based taco meat with chili powder and garlic and simmer it with onion, tomato sauce, and a splash of vegetable broth until the mixture thickens but is still nice and saucy. Brown sugar and cider vinegar add sweet-tangy depth to the mixture. Romaine lettuce hearts, black beans, and juicy cherry tomatoes make up the salad portion of the dish. There's no need for a separate dressing; in combination with fresh lime juice, the sauce from the meat mixture provides plenty of flavor and ties all the components together. A garnish of crumbled tortilla chips adds welcome crunch. Serve with your favorite taco toppings.

1 for the taco meat: Heat oil in 12-inch nonstick skillet over medium heat until shimmering. Add onion and salt and cook until softened and beginning to brown, 5 to 7 minutes. Stir in ground meat and cook, breaking up meat with wooden spoon, until firm crumbles form, about 3 minutes. Stir in chili powder and garlic and cook until fragrant, about 30 seconds.

2 Stir in tomato sauce, broth, vinegar, and sugar and simmer until slightly thickened, about 5 minutes. Off heat, season with salt and pepper to taste.

3 for the salad: Combine lettuce, beans, tomatoes, scallions, and ¼ cup cilantro in large bowl; toss with lime juice and season with salt and pepper to taste. Divide salad among serving bowls, then top bowls with taco meat, tortilla chips, and remaining ¼ cup cilantro. Serve with lime wedges.

lemony brown rice bowl with meatballs and sun-dried tomatoes

serves 4

total time 1¼ hours

½ cup panko bread crumbs

4 scallions, white and green parts separated and sliced thin, greens divided

¼ cup chopped fresh parsley, divided

2 tablespoons plus 2 cups water, divided

2 teaspoons grated lemon zest, divided, plus 2 tablespoons juice

¼ teaspoon table salt

⅛ teaspoon pepper

12 ounces plant-based ground meat

1 tablespoon extra-virgin olive oil

1 cup long-grain brown rice, rinsed

3 garlic cloves, minced

2 cups vegetable broth

½ cup oil-packed sun-dried tomatoes, rinsed, patted dry, and sliced thin

why this recipe works This meal of herbed meatballs and nutty brown rice is an archetypal example of the one-pan dinner genre—a pantry-friendly, easy, and flavorful dish that gets right to the point with no fuss. To give the meatballs a brighter, lighter profile, we mix the plant-based meat with fresh herbs and lemon zest. We brown the meatballs all over to build up a nice crusty exterior and create some fond and then, to prevent the meatballs from overcooking, we remove them from the pan while we soften the aromatics. We give the rice a head start in vegetable broth infused with more lemon zest and a squeeze of lemon juice and then nestle the meatballs into the gently simmering rice, cover, and let the dish finish cooking through, hands-off. Sun-dried tomatoes add color and chewy savor, and last-minute sprinkles of parsley and scallion greens finish the dish on a fresh note. You will need a 12-inch nonstick skillet with a tight-fitting lid.

1 Stir panko, 2 tablespoons scallion greens, 2 tablespoons parsley, 2 tablespoons water, 1½ teaspoons lemon zest, salt, and pepper in large bowl until evenly combined. Break ground meat into small pieces and add to bowl with panko mixture. Gently knead with your hands until mixture is well combined. Using your moistened hands, pinch off and roll meat mixture into 1½-inch meatballs. (You should have 12 meatballs.) Transfer meatballs to plate and refrigerate for at least 15 minutes or up to 24 hours.

2 Heat oil in 12-inch nonstick skillet over medium-high heat until shimmering. Add meatballs and cook until well browned all over, 2 to 3 minutes. Transfer meatballs to large plate.

3 Cook rice in now-empty skillet over medium-high heat until edges of rice begin to turn translucent, about 1 minute. Add garlic and scallion whites and cook until fragrant, about 1 minute. Stir in broth, remaining 2 cups water, lemon juice, and remaining ½ teaspoon lemon zest and bring to boil.

4 Reduce heat to medium-low, cover, and cook for 15 minutes. Nestle meatballs into skillet, cover, and cook until rice is tender and no liquid remains, 15 to 25 minutes. Off heat, scatter sun-dried tomatoes over top and let sit, covered, for 5 minutes. Sprinkle with remaining scallion greens and remaining 2 tablespoons parsley. Serve.

quinoa bowl with meatballs, green beans, and garlic dressing

serves 4
total time 1 hour

dressing

- 3 tablespoons roasted garlic cloves
- 2 tablespoons white wine vinegar
- 1 teaspoon maple syrup or honey
- ½ teaspoon Dijon mustard
- ½ teaspoon minced fresh thyme
- ⅛ teaspoon table salt
- ⅛ teaspoon pepper
- 3 tablespoons extra-virgin olive oil

bowls

- ½ cup panko bread crumbs
- ¼ cup chopped fresh parsley
- 1½ teaspoons ground fennel
- 1½ teaspoons ground sage
- ¾ teaspoon plus ⅛ teaspoon table salt, divided
- ⅛ teaspoon pepper
- 12 ounces plant-based ground meat
- 1¼ cups prewashed white quinoa
- 4 teaspoons extra-virgin olive oil, divided
- 8 ounces green beans, trimmed and halved crosswise
- ¼ cup dried cranberries
- ¼ cup sliced almonds, toasted

why this recipe works This hearty grain bowl distills the essence of Thanksgiving dinner into an easy plant-based feast. In lieu of turkey, we use plant-based meatballs flavored with parsley, ground fennel, and ground sage. Rather than a bread stuffing, we cook nutty quinoa to use as the bowl's base. Green beans take just a few minutes in a skillet to turn crisp-tender, and a handful of dried cranberries adds chewy tartness. To tie the bowl together, we drizzle our homemade creamy roasted garlic dressing liberally over everything. You can often find roasted garlic in your supermarket's olive bar section. If roasted garlic is unavailable, you can make your own: Cut the top third off two heads of garlic and wrap tightly in aluminum foil. Roast the garlic in a 350-degree oven until very tender, about 1 hour. When the garlic is cool enough to handle, squeeze the cloves from the skins and discard the skins.

1 for the dressing: Process garlic, vinegar, 1½ tablespoons water, maple syrup, mustard, thyme, salt, and pepper in blender until smooth, about 45 seconds, scraping down sides of blender jar as needed. With blender running, slowly add oil until combined, about 1 minute. Season with salt and pepper to taste. (Dressing can be refrigerated for up to 1 week; whisk to recombine before serving.)

2 for the bowls: Stir 2 tablespoons water, panko, parsley, fennel, sage, ¼ teaspoon salt, and pepper in large bowl until evenly combined. Break ground meat into small pieces and add to bowl with panko mixture. Gently knead with your hands until mixture is well combined. Using your moistened hands, pinch off and roll meat mixture into ¾-inch meatballs. (You should have 24 meatballs.) Transfer meatballs to plate and refrigerate for at least 15 minutes or up to 24 hours.

3 Meanwhile, toast quinoa in medium saucepan over medium-high heat, stirring frequently, until very fragrant and makes continuous popping sound, 5 to 7 minutes. Stir in 1¾ cups water and ½ teaspoon salt and bring to simmer. Reduce heat to low, cover, and simmer until quinoa is tender and water is absorbed, 18 to 22 minutes, stirring once halfway through cooking.

4 Remove pot from heat and let sit, covered, for 10 minutes, then gently fluff with fork. Season with salt and pepper to taste.

5 Heat 2 teaspoons oil in 12-inch nonstick skillet over medium heat until shimmering. Add meatballs and cook, turning frequently, until browned on all sides and firm, 5 to 7 minutes. Transfer meatballs to clean plate, cover with aluminum foil to keep warm, and set aside until ready to serve. Heat remaining 2 teaspoons oil in now-empty skillet over medium-high heat until shimmering. Add green beans and remaining ⅛ teaspoon salt and cook until green beans are spotty brown, 2 to 4 minutes.

6 Divide quinoa among individual serving bowls, then top with meatballs and green beans. Drizzle with dressing and sprinkle with cranberries and almonds. Serve.

farro bowl with butternut squash, sausage, and radicchio

serves 4 to 6
total time 1¼ hours

2	pounds butternut squash, peeled, seeded, and cut into ½-inch pieces (7 cups)
½	cup extra-virgin olive oil, divided
¾	teaspoon table salt, divided, plus salt for cooking farro
¾	teaspoon pepper, divided
1½	cups whole farro
12	ounces plant-based ground meat
1	recipe Sweet Italian Sausage Seasoning (page 11)
3	garlic cloves, minced
¼	cup balsamic vinegar
2	teaspoons Dijon mustard
1	head radicchio (10 ounces), cored and cut into 1-inch pieces
½	cup fresh parsley leaves
8	fresh figs, halved and sliced thin
2	ounces plant-based or dairy blue cheese, crumbled (½ cup) (optional)

why this recipe works Most of us don't have the luxury of taking regular strolls through the food markets of Tuscany in late September, but that doesn't mean we can't enjoy Italian autumnal flavors at home. This bowl showcases the bounty of an Italian harvest with crunchy, bitter radicchio and sweet roasted butternut squash over a base of nutty, pleasantly chewy farro (an ancient Mediterranean grain beloved in Italy). Gorgeous ripe figs give the bowl a honeyed sweetness that's balanced by the piquant Dijon–balsamic vinegar dressing. In keeping with the theme, we combine our homemade Italian sausage seasoning with plant-based meat and top each bowl with the resulting sausagey, savory crumbles. The blue cheese adds luxe creaminess and earthy funk, but there's so much going on in these bountiful bowls that you won't miss it if omitted. Any type of fresh fig will work in this recipe. You can substitute 1½ cups seedless grapes, quartered, for the figs, if desired.

1 Adjust oven rack to lowest position and heat oven to 450 degrees. Line rimmed baking sheet with aluminum foil. Toss squash with 1 tablespoon oil, ¼ teaspoon salt, and ¼ teaspoon pepper and spread in even layer on prepared sheet. Roast until well browned and tender, 30 to 35 minutes, stirring once halfway through cooking.

2 Meanwhile, bring 4 quarts water to boil in large pot. Add farro and 1 tablespoon salt and cook until tender, 15 to 30 minutes. Drain well.

3 Heat 1 tablespoon oil in 12-inch nonstick skillet over medium heat until shimmering. Add ground meat and cook, breaking up meat with wooden spoon, until firm crumbles form, about 3 minutes. Stir in Italian sausage seasoning and garlic and cook until fragrant, about 30 seconds; transfer to bowl.

4 Whisk vinegar, mustard, remaining ½ teaspoon salt, and remaining ½ teaspoon pepper together in bowl. While whisking constantly, slowly drizzle in remaining 6 tablespoons oil until combined. Toss radicchio, parsley, and farro with half of vinaigrette to coat, then season with salt and pepper to taste. Divide among individual serving bowls, then top with meat mixture; squash; figs; and blue cheese, if using. Drizzle with remaining vinaigrette. Serve.

chapter 4

soup-pot, skillet, and sheet-pan meals

italian wedding soup

<table>
<tr><td>serves 4 to 6</td></tr>
<tr><td>total time 1¼ hours</td></tr>
</table>

broth

- 1 tablespoon extra-virgin olive oil
- 1 fennel bulb, stalks discarded, bulb halved, cored, and chopped
- 1 onion, chopped
- 4 garlic cloves, smashed and peeled
- ¼ ounce dried porcini mushrooms, rinsed
- ½ cup dry white wine
- 1 tablespoon plant-based or traditional Worcestershire sauce
- 4 cups vegetable broth

meatballs

- ½ cup panko bread crumbs
- 4 teaspoons finely grated onion
- ¾ teaspoon dried oregano
- ½ teaspoon garlic, minced to paste
- ¼ teaspoon ground fennel
- ¼ teaspoon table salt
- ⅛ teaspoon pepper
- 12 ounces plant-based ground meat
- 12 ounces kale, stemmed and cut into ½-inch pieces (6 cups)
- 2 carrots, peeled and sliced thin on bias
- 5 ounces ditalini

  Plant-based or dairy Parmesan cheese (optional)

why this recipe works Italian wedding soup is so named because the meatballs, greens, and pasta live in a harmonious "marriage" in a savory broth. Because the broth is the unifying element, we start there, simmering vegetable broth, water, and white wine with aromatic fennel, onion, garlic, and umami-rich dried porcini mushrooms. While the broth simmers, we move on to the plant-based meatballs, boosting their flavor with onion, garlic, dried oregano, and ground fennel and gently poaching them in the broth until deliciously tender. Assertive, sturdy chopped kale acts as a counterpoint to the tender meatballs, a handful of chopped carrots adds sweetness and cheerful orange pops of color, and dainty ditalini give each bite satisfying wheaty chew. A rasp-style grater makes quick work of grating the onion; you can also use it to easily turn the garlic into a paste. You can substitute tubettini or orzo for the ditalini. You can use store-bought Parmesan or make our Plant-Based Parmesan (page 12), if desired.

1 for the broth: Heat oil in Dutch oven over medium-high heat until shimmering. Add fennel, onion, garlic, and mushrooms and cook, stirring frequently, until just softened and beginning to brown, 5 to 7 minutes. Stir in wine and Worcestershire and cook for 1 minute. Stir in broth and 4 cups water and bring to boil. Reduce heat to low, cover, and simmer for 30 minutes.

2 for the meatballs: While broth simmers, stir panko, 2 tablespoons water, onion, oregano, garlic, ground fennel, salt, and pepper in large bowl until evenly combined. Break ground meat into small pieces and add to bowl with panko mixture. Gently knead with your hands until mixture is well combined. Using your moistened hands, pinch off and roll meat mixture into ¾-inch meatballs. (You should have 25 to 30 meatballs.) Transfer meatballs to plate and refrigerate for at least 15 minutes or up to 24 hours.

3 Strain broth through fine-mesh strainer set over large bowl, pressing on solids to extract as much broth as possible; discard solids.

4 Return broth to clean, dry pot and bring to simmer over medium-high heat. Add kale, carrots, and pasta and cook, stirring occasionally, for 5 minutes. Add meatballs, return to simmer, and cook, gently stirring occasionally, until meatballs are firm and pasta is tender, about 5 minutes. Season with salt and pepper to taste. Serve with Parmesan, if using.

kimchi, meat, and tofu soup

serves 4 to 6
total time 40 minutes

2   teaspoons vegetable oil

12 ounces plant-based
    ground meat

¼   teaspoon table salt

½   teaspoon pepper

1   tablespoon grated
    fresh ginger

3   cups water

3   cups kimchi, drained with
    ¼ cup brine reserved,
    chopped coarse

2   cups vegetable broth

8   ounces firm tofu, cut into
    ½-inch pieces

½   cup mirin

2   tablespoons soy sauce

4   scallions, sliced thin

1   tablespoon toasted
    sesame oil

why this recipe works Kimchi stew can be found on dinner tables across Korea in an almost limitless number of variations. All of these variations share a warming, tangy depth that inspired us to develop this plant-based soup. We first cook the plant-based meat with a little oil until a thin fond forms on the bottom of the pot, later scraping up and stirring those browned bits back into the broth to intensify the soup's savor. Kimchi lends the soup its spicy tang, and aromatic ginger, mirin, and soy sauce round out the broth's flavors. Using firm tofu ensures that the cubes hold together when stirred into the soup along with the broth. A garnish of scallions and toasted sesame oil finishes each serving with freshness and complex nuttiness. Make sure to save the kimchi brine when draining the kimchi. If there's not enough brine in the jar to yield ¼ cup, add water to compensate. Note that the flavor and spiciness of kimchi can vary from brand to brand. Make sure to use firm or extra-firm (not soft) tofu here.

1 Heat vegetable oil in Dutch oven over medium heat until shimmering. Add ground meat, salt, and pepper and cook, breaking up meat with wooden spoon, until firm crumbles form, about 3 minutes.

2 Add ginger and cook until fragrant, about 30 seconds. Stir in water, kimchi and reserved brine, broth, tofu, mirin, and soy sauce. Scrape up browned bits on bottom of pot using metal spatula or wooden spoon. Bring to boil, then reduce heat to low, cover, and simmer for 15 minutes.

3 Off heat, stir in scallions and toasted sesame oil. Serve.

green chile stew with hominy

serves 4
total time 45 minutes

- 2 teaspoons vegetable oil
- 1 large onion, chopped fine
- 2 poblano chiles, stemmed, seeded, and chopped
- 2 jalapeño chiles, stemmed, seeded, and minced
- 12 ounces plant-based ground meat
- 4 garlic cloves, minced
- 1 teaspoon ground cumin
- 2 (12-ounce) cans whole tomatillos, drained
- 3½ cups vegetable broth
- 2 (15-ounce) cans white hominy, rinsed
- 2 tomatoes, cored and cut into ½-inch pieces
- 2 radishes, trimmed, halved, and sliced thin
- ½ cup fresh cilantro leaves

why this recipe works Mexican green pozole is traditionally a long-simmered pork and hominy stew. Although many typical recipes call for pork shoulder, in the past we've found that we could quicken the process by using ground pork—so when it came to our meat-free adaptation, we were confident that we could substitute plant-based ground meat for the pork in our weeknight-friendly recipe. Two types of chile peppers—poblano and jalapeño—give the stew complex spiciness; we soften the chiles along with an onion and then add the meat, which takes just a few minutes to cook through. Tomatillos are the base of a classic green pozole, so next we stir in two cans of mashed tomatillos, broth to thin the stew's consistency, and a couple cans of hominy (corn kernels treated with an alkali to soften their tough hulls). We simmer the lot until the flavors meld, crowning each steaming bowl with chopped tomatoes, sliced radishes, and cilantro leaves.

1 Heat oil in Dutch oven over medium heat until shimmering. Add onion, poblanos, and jalapeños and cook until softened and lightly browned, 5 to 7 minutes. Add ground meat and cook, breaking up meat with wooden spoon, until firm crumbles form, about 3 minutes.

2 Stir in garlic and cumin and cook until fragrant, about 1 minute. Mash tomatillos coarse in bowl using potato masher, then add to pot along with broth and hominy. Scrape up browned bits on bottom of pot using metal spatula or wooden spoon and bring to simmer.

3 Cook, stirring occasionally, until stew is slightly thickened, about 15 minutes. Season with salt and pepper to taste. Serve, topping individual bowls with tomatoes, radishes, and cilantro.

weeknight meaty chili

serves 6 to 8
total time 50 minutes

2 tablespoons vegetable oil

2 onions, chopped fine

2 red bell peppers, stemmed, seeded, and chopped

4 garlic cloves, minced

1 tablespoon chili powder

2 teaspoons ground cumin

1–2 teaspoons minced canned chipotle chile in adobo sauce

½ teaspoon dried oregano

½ teaspoon table salt

¼ teaspoon pepper

12 ounces plant-based ground meat

2 (15-ounce) cans kidney beans, rinsed

1 (28-ounce) can whole peeled tomatoes, drained with juice reserved, chopped fine

1 (15-ounce) can tomato sauce

1 cup water

why this recipe works This speedy, family-friendly chili is a win-win for everyone. To create a chili that feels familiar (nostalgic, even) using plant-based meat, we build aromatic flavors from onion, garlic, and red bell peppers (which we chop coarse for a hearty texture) before cooking the plant-based meat just until it begins forming firm crumbles, a sign that it's cooked through. Chili powder, cumin, and oregano bring intense earthy fragrance, while chipotle chile contributes smoky heat. Convenient canned kidney beans bulk up the chili, while tomato sauce and chopped whole peeled tomatoes give the chili a great saucy-chunky texture. Use the lesser amount of chipotle chile if you prefer a milder level of spiciness. Load up the chili with all your favorite toppings for serving.

1 Heat oil in Dutch oven over medium heat until shimmering. Add onions, bell peppers, garlic, chili powder, cumin, chipotle, oregano, salt, and pepper and cook, stirring frequently, until vegetables are softened, 8 to 10 minutes.

2 Stir in ground meat and cook, breaking up meat with wooden spoon, until firm crumbles form, about 3 minutes. Stir in beans, tomatoes and reserved juice, tomato sauce, and water. Scrape up browned bits on bottom of pot using metal spatula or wooden spoon.

3 Bring to simmer, then reduce heat to low and simmer until chili thickens slightly, 15 to 20 minutes. Season with salt and pepper to taste, and serve.

black bean, sweet potato, and zucchini chili

serves 6 to 8
total time 1¼ hours

3 tablespoons vegetable oil

1 pound sweet potatoes, peeled and cut into ½-inch pieces

1 onion, chopped

2 tablespoons chili powder

3 garlic cloves, minced

1 teaspoon ground cumin

1 (28-ounce) can diced tomatoes

1½ cups mild lager, such as Budweiser

½ teaspoon table salt

2 (15-ounce) cans black beans, rinsed

1 zucchini, quartered lengthwise and sliced crosswise ¼ inch thick

12 ounces plant-based ground meat

4 scallions, sliced thin

¼ cup roasted pepitas

Lime wedges

why this recipe works If a meaty chili and a wholesome vegetable stew had a baby, the result would be this layered, vegetable-forward chili bursting with sweet potatoes, zucchini, black beans, and plant-based meat. Since the dense sweet potatoes take the longest to break down and become tender, we start by cutting them into small pieces and softening them in a Dutch oven along with an onion. Chili powder, garlic, and cumin amp up the chili's flavor and add a touch of heat to balance the sweetness from the spuds. Beer and a can of diced tomatoes act as the liquid component. Once the sweet potatoes are tender, we stir in canned black beans and zucchini and then add the plant-based meat, breaking the meat into substantial pieces so that its identity comes through clearly among all the veg. A sprinkling of scallions and roasted pepitas add textural contrast, and a squeeze of lime juice is just the thing for tempering this rustic chili's richness.

1 Heat oil in Dutch oven over medium-high heat until shimmering. Add sweet potatoes and onion and cook until onion is softened and beginning to brown, 7 to 10 minutes. Stir in chili powder, garlic, and cumin and cook until fragrant, about 30 seconds.

2 Stir in tomatoes and their juice, beer, and salt, scraping up browned bits on bottom of pot using metal spatula or wooden spoon. Bring to simmer, then reduce heat to medium-low, cover, and cook, stirring occasionally, until sweet potatoes are just tender, about 20 minutes.

3 Stir in black beans and zucchini. Gently stir ground meat into pot, pinching off meat into pieces no smaller than ½ inch, and bring to simmer. Cook, uncovered, until zucchini is tender, 15 to 20 minutes. Season with salt and pepper to taste. Sprinkle individual portions with scallions and pepitas. Serve with lime wedges.

skillet chipotle chili with lime-cilantro crema

serves 4 to 6
total time 1 hour

½ cup plain plant-based or dairy Greek yogurt

¼ cup minced fresh cilantro, divided

2 teaspoons grated lime zest, divided, plus 3 tablespoons juice (2 limes), divided

1¼ teaspoons table salt, divided

2 tablespoons vegetable oil, divided

1 cup long-grain white rice, rinsed

2 cups water

1 onion, chopped fine

1 red bell pepper, stemmed, seeded, and chopped

Pinch pepper

12 ounces plant-based ground meat

1 tablespoon ground cumin

2 garlic cloves, minced

2 teaspoons chipotle chile powder

1 (15-ounce) can tomato sauce

1 (15-ounce) can black beans, rinsed

1 cup frozen corn, thawed

why this recipe works Chili made in a skillet? You bet! Cooking in stages in our hard-working nonstick skillet brings together a one-pan dinner of saucy, smoky chili and fluffy rice with minimal fuss. We start by toasting and simmering the rice, flavoring it with lime zest and juice to brighten it up; toasting the rice gives it an irresistible nuttiness and helps prevent the grains from sticking together. When the rice is done, we transfer it to a bowl and cover it with aluminum foil to keep warm. We then brown the plant-based meat and vegetable base of the chili in the same skillet. Blooming ground cumin and chipotle chile powder with minced garlic boosts the spices' potency before we stir in tomato sauce, black beans, and corn. A lime-cilantro yogurt sauce finishes off each bowl with creamy, zesty pizzazz. You will need a 12-inch nonstick skillet with a tight-fitting lid. Serve with sliced jalapeños, shredded cheese, and diced avocado, if desired.

1 Whisk yogurt, 2 tablespoons cilantro, 1 teaspoon lime zest and 1 tablespoon lime juice, and ¼ teaspoon salt together in bowl; cover and refrigerate yogurt sauce until ready to serve.

2 Meanwhile, heat 1 tablespoon oil in 12-inch nonstick skillet over medium heat until shimmering. Add rice and cook, stirring often, until edges of rice begin to turn translucent, about 2 minutes. Add water and ½ teaspoon salt and bring to boil. Cover, reduce heat to low, and simmer until liquid is absorbed and rice is tender, about 20 minutes.

3 Off heat, add remaining 1 teaspoon lime zest and remaining 2 tablespoons lime juice and fluff gently with fork to incorporate. Transfer to bowl and cover with aluminum foil to keep warm.

4 Heat remaining 1 tablespoon oil in now-empty skillet over medium heat until shimmering. Add onion, bell pepper, pepper, and remaining ½ teaspoon salt and cook until vegetables are just beginning to brown, 5 to 7 minutes. Add ground meat and cook, breaking up meat with wooden spoon, until firm crumbles form, about 3 minutes.

5 Stir in cumin, garlic, and chile powder and cook until fragrant, about 1 minute. Stir in tomato sauce, beans, and corn and cook until most of liquid is absorbed, about 2 minutes. Serve chili over rice with yogurt sauce and remaining 2 tablespoons cilantro.

mapo tofu

serves 4 to 6
total time 40 minutes

1 tablespoon Sichuan peppercorns

12 scallions

1¾ pounds soft tofu, cut into ½-inch pieces

2 cups vegetable broth

⅓ cup broad bean chili paste

1 (3-inch) piece ginger, peeled and cut into ¼-inch-thick rounds

9 garlic cloves, peeled

1 tablespoon fermented black beans

6 tablespoons vegetable oil, divided

1 tablespoon Sichuan chili powder

8 ounces plant-based ground meat

2 tablespoons hoisin sauce

2 teaspoons toasted sesame oil

2 tablespoons water

1 tablespoon cornstarch

why this recipe works This Sichuan dish of braised tofu features a heady amalgam of savory fermented chili paste and black beans, ginger, garlic, sweet hoisin, toasted sesame oil, and mouth-tingling Sichuan peppercorns. The addition of ground beef (or in this case, plant-based meat) gives the dish its delectable meatiness. We poach the soft cubes of tofu in vegetable broth to firm their exteriors so they stay intact. After cooking the meat and spice paste, we scrape the flavorful browned bits that form on the bottom of the pan back into the sauce. Thickening the sauce with cornstarch gives it a velvety, clingy texture. Broad bean chili paste (or sauce) is also known as doubanjiang or toban djan. Lee Kum Kee Chili Bean Sauce is a good supermarket option. If you can't find fermented black beans, you can use 1 teaspoon of fermented black bean paste or sauce or 2 additional teaspoons of broad bean chili paste. Serve with rice.

1 Microwave peppercorns until fragrant, 15 to 30 seconds. Let cool completely, then grind using spice grinder or mortar and pestle until finely ground (you should have 1½ teaspoons); set aside. Using side of chef's knife, lightly crush white parts of scallions, then cut scallions into 1-inch pieces. Microwave scallions, tofu, and broth in large covered bowl until steaming, 5 to 7 minutes; set aside.

2 Process chili paste, ginger, garlic, and black beans in food processor until coarse paste forms, 1 to 2 minutes, scraping down sides of bowl as needed. Add ¼ cup vegetable oil, chili powder, and 1 teaspoon reserved peppercorns and process until smooth paste forms, 1 to 2 minutes; set aside.

3 Heat 1 tablespoon vegetable oil in large saucepan over medium heat until shimmering. Add ground meat and cook, breaking up meat with wooden spoon, until firm crumbles form, about 3 minutes. Using slotted spoon, transfer meat to bowl.

4 Add remaining 1 tablespoon vegetable oil and reserved spice paste to now-empty saucepan and cook, stirring frequently, until paste darkens and oil begins to separate from paste, 2 to 3 minutes. Gently pour reserved tofu mixture into saucepan, followed by hoisin, sesame oil, and meat. Scrape up browned bits on bottom of saucepan using metal spatula or wooden spoon and cook until mixture comes to simmer, 2 to 3 minutes.

5 Whisk water and cornstarch together in small bowl, then add to saucepan and continue to cook, stirring frequently, until thickened, 2 to 3 minutes longer. Sprinkle with remaining ½ teaspoon reserved peppercorns. Serve.

keema

serves 4 to 6
total time 50 minutes

2 tablespoons vegetable oil

6 black peppercorns

4 green cardamom pods

2 black cardamom pods

1 cinnamon stick

1 red onion, halved and sliced thin crosswise

1 teaspoon grated garlic

1 teaspoon grated fresh ginger

12 ounces plant-based ground meat

¾ teaspoon table salt

2 teaspoons ground coriander

2 teaspoons Kashmiri chile powder

½ teaspoon ground turmeric

½ teaspoon ground cumin

12 ounces tomatoes, cored and chopped

¼ cup plain plant-based or dairy yogurt

1 long green chile, halved lengthwise (optional)

6 tablespoons chopped fresh cilantro, divided

why this recipe works A rich and savory spiced dish that's been a staple of Indian cuisine for centuries, keema features ground or minced meat simmered in a fragrant sauce. Here we bloom whole spices in oil to coax out their flavors and make a potent homemade garam masala. After cooking plant-based meat with red onion, garlic, and ginger, we add more spices, chopped fresh tomatoes, and yogurt, simmering everything together until the flavors meld and the sauce thickens. The delectable results are ideal for scooping up with naan. Kashmiri chile powder gives the keema its vivid color and subtle heat; if you can't find it, toast and grind one large guajillo chile and substitute 2 teaspoons guajillo chile powder for the Kashmiri chile powder. To toast a dried chile quickly, microwave at full power in 10-second intervals until the chile is hot to the touch, slightly darkened, and pliable. Look for black and green cardamom pods, Kashmiri chile powder, and 4- to 5-inch long Indian green chiles at Indian or Pakistani markets. Any long green chile, including jalapeño, serrano, or Thai chile, will work depending on how spicy you want the final dish to be. For a milder keema, omit the fresh chile or use only half of it. Use a rasp-style grater to grate the garlic and ginger. Serve with naan, roti, or basmati rice.

1 Heat oil in medium saucepan over medium heat until shimmering. Add peppercorns, green and black cardamom pods, and cinnamon stick and cook, stirring occasionally, until fragrant, about 30 seconds. Add onion and cook, stirring occasionally, until onion is browned, 7 to 10 minutes.

2 Add garlic and ginger and cook, stirring constantly, until fragrant, about 30 seconds. Increase heat to medium-high, add ground meat and salt, and cook, breaking up meat into very small pieces with wooden spoon, until firm crumbles form, about 3 minutes.

3 Add coriander, chile powder, turmeric, and cumin and cook, stirring constantly, until fragrant, about 1 minute. Add tomatoes; yogurt; and chile, if using, and cook, stirring frequently, until tomatoes release their juice and mixture begins to simmer, about 2 minutes.

4 Adjust heat to maintain gentle simmer. Cover and cook, stirring occasionally, until tomatoes have broken down and wooden spoon scraped across bottom of saucepan leaves clear trail, 12 to 18 minutes. Stir in ¼ cup cilantro and season with salt and pepper to taste. If desired, remove cinnamon stick and cardamom pods. Transfer to serving bowl, sprinkle with remaining 2 tablespoons cilantro, and serve.

cuban picadillo

serves 4 to 6
total time 50 minutes

1 green bell pepper, stemmed, seeded, and chopped coarse

1 onion, chopped coarse

1 (14.5-ounce) can whole peeled tomatoes, drained

2 tablespoons vegetable oil

1 tablespoon dried oregano

1 tablespoon ground cumin

½ teaspoon ground cinnamon

¼ teaspoon table salt

6 garlic cloves, minced

¾ cup dry white wine

½ cup vegetable broth

½ cup raisins

3 bay leaves

12 ounces plant-based ground meat

½ cup pimento-stuffed green olives, chopped coarse

2 tablespoons capers, rinsed

1 tablespoon red wine vinegar, plus extra for seasoning

why this recipe works Traditional Cuban picadillo is a one-pot dish featuring finely chopped beef and a balanced sweet-sour-savory flavor profile. Our rendition begins with chopping the vegetables (bell pepper and onion) and blooming the spices (oregano, cumin, and cinnamon) in oil. We then build the sauce by adding canned tomatoes, white wine, and vegetable broth; the tomatoes and wine give the picadillo its characteristic subtle tartness. Raisins and olives are typical additions, and we also like the brininess provided by capers and the extra brightness from a splash of red wine vinegar. While many of our recipes for plant-based meat call for browning the meat to develop a nice charred flavor, here we skip that step, simmering it gently in the sauce for juicy tenderness. Serve with rice and black beans and top with chopped parsley, toasted sliced almonds, and/or chopped hard-cooked egg, if you like.

1 Pulse bell pepper and onion in food processor until chopped into ¼-inch pieces, about 12 pulses; transfer to bowl. Pulse tomatoes in food processor until coarsely chopped, about 5 pulses.

2 Heat oil in Dutch oven over medium-high heat until shimmering. Add oregano, cumin, cinnamon, salt, and pepper-onion mixture and cook, stirring frequently, until vegetables are softened and beginning to brown, 6 to 8 minutes. Stir in garlic and cook until fragrant, about 30 seconds. Stir in wine and tomatoes and cook, scraping up browned bits on bottom of pot using metal spatula or wooden spoon, until pot is almost dry, 3 to 5 minutes. Stir in broth, raisins, and bay leaves and bring to simmer.

3 Reduce heat to medium-low. Add ground meat to pot, pinching off meat into pieces no smaller than ¼ inch, and bring to simmer. Cook, covered, stirring occasionally, until meat is firm, about 5 minutes.

4 Discard bay leaves. Stir in olives and capers. Increase heat to medium-high and cook, stirring occasionally, until most of liquid has evaporated, about 2 minutes. Stir in vinegar and season with salt, pepper, and extra vinegar to taste. Serve.

one-pot rice and lentils with spiced meat

serves 6
total time 1¼ hours

yogurt sauce

- 1 cup plain plant-based or dairy yogurt
- 2 tablespoons lemon juice
- ½ teaspoon minced garlic
- ½ teaspoon table salt

rice, lentils, and spiced meat

- 1¼ cups basmati rice
- 3 tablespoons extra-virgin olive oil
- 12 ounces plant-based ground meat
- 3 garlic cloves, minced
- 1 teaspoon ground coriander
- 1 teaspoon ground cumin
- ½ teaspoon ground cinnamon
- ½ teaspoon ground allspice
- ¼ teaspoon pepper
- ⅛ teaspoon cayenne pepper
- 1 teaspoon sugar
- 1 teaspoon table salt
- 1 (15-ounce) can lentils, rinsed
- 1½ cups crispy onions, divided
- 3 tablespoons minced fresh dill

why this recipe works Our jumping-off point for this meaty take on rice and beans is mujaddara, a dish served across the eastern Mediterranean that exemplifies how a few humble ingredients (spiced rice, lentils, crispy onions, and yogurt sauce) can add up to something spectacular. A classic mujaddara calls for frying onions from scratch, but in the name of simplifying matters we opt for store-bought crispy onions. And while most mujaddaras don't include meat, here we like the way plant-based meat adds heartiness and savory depth. To ensure that the pilaf turns out light and fluffy, we soak basmati rice in hot water to eliminate its excess sticky starch and then add it to the pot with the meat along with copious amounts of warm spices. After a quick toasting, in go the water and lentils to simmer until everything is cooked. Any long-grain white rice can be substituted for the basmati.

1 for the yogurt sauce: Whisk all ingredients together in bowl. Refrigerate until ready to serve.

2 for the rice, lentils, and spiced meat: Place rice in medium bowl and cover with hot water by 2 inches; let sit for 15 minutes.

3 Using your hands, gently swish rice grains to release excess starch. Carefully pour off water, leaving rice in bowl. Add cold water to rice and pour off water. Repeat adding and pouring off cold water 4 or 5 times, until water runs almost clear. Drain rice in fine-mesh strainer.

4 Heat oil in Dutch oven over medium heat until shimmering. Add ground meat and cook, breaking up meat with wooden spoon, until firm crumbles form, about 3 minutes. Add garlic, coriander, cumin, cinnamon, allspice, pepper, and cayenne and cook until fragrant, about 30 seconds. Add rice and cook, stirring occasionally, until edges of rice begin to turn translucent, about 3 minutes. Add 2¼ cups water, sugar, and salt and bring to boil, scraping up browned bits with metal spatula or wooden spoon. Stir in lentils, reduce heat to low, cover, and cook until rice is tender and all liquid is absorbed, about 12 minutes.

5 Off heat, lay clean dish towel underneath lid and let sit for 10 minutes. Fluff rice and lentils with fork and stir in half of crispy onions; season with salt and pepper to taste. Transfer to serving platter, top with dill and remaining crispy onions, and serve, passing yogurt sauce separately.

sautéed eggplant
with polenta

serves 4
total time 1 hour

1 (12-ounce) eggplant, trimmed, halved crosswise, and cut into 1-inch-thick wedges

1 onion, halved and sliced thin

5½ cups water, divided

6 tablespoons extra-virgin olive oil, divided

4 garlic cloves, sliced thin

1 teaspoon table salt, divided

12 ounces plant-based ground meat

1 cup instant polenta

2 cups canned crushed tomatoes

¼ cup golden raisins

¼ cup pitted kalamata olives, chopped

1 tablespoon capers, rinsed

¼ teaspoon red pepper flakes

1 tablespoon chopped fresh parsley

why this recipe works Combine the lush meatiness of a Southern Italian ragù with the silky pungency of a Sicilian caponata, and the result is this extraordinary mash-up. Here, the tomatoey meat sauce mingles with tender bites of stewed eggplant, and all is served atop a pillow of golden polenta (a common pairing for ragù). Using quick-cooking plant-based meat and instant polenta means the whole thing can be made start to finish in an hour. We first cut the eggplant into thick wedges and gently braise it in a small amount of water flavored with onion, olive oil, and garlic, allowing the eggplant to soak up the braising liquid's flavors like a sponge. Once the liquid cooks off and the eggplant browns, we stir in the meat, followed by canned tomatoes, raisins, olives, and capers to complete the potent sauce. All that's left is to spoon the sauce on top of individual servings of the hearty polenta and dig in. Large eggplants disintegrate when braised; using a smaller eggplant ensures that the wedges stay intact.

1 Cook eggplant, onion, ½ cup water, ¼ cup oil, garlic, and ¼ teaspoon salt in 12-inch nonstick skillet, covered, over medium-high heat, stirring occasionally, until water has evaporated and vegetables are softened, about 10 minutes. Uncover and continue to cook, stirring often, until eggplant and onion are lightly browned, about 8 minutes. Add ground meat and cook, breaking up meat with wooden spoon, until firm crumbles form, about 3 minutes.

2 Meanwhile, bring remaining 5 cups water to boil in large saucepan over medium-high heat. Slowly add polenta while whisking constantly. Reduce heat to medium-low and cook until thickened, about 3 minutes. Off heat, stir in remaining 2 tablespoons oil and remaining ¾ teaspoon salt.

3 Stir tomatoes, raisins, olives, capers, and pepper flakes into eggplant-meat mixture and bring to boil. Reduce heat to medium-low and simmer until slightly thickened, about 8 minutes. Season with salt and pepper to taste. Sprinkle with parsley and serve with polenta.

sautéed eggplant with soy, ginger, and scallions

serves 4
total time 35 minutes

¼ cup vegetable oil, divided

1½ pounds eggplant, cut into 1-inch pieces

2 tablespoons soy sauce, divided

12 ounces plant-based ground meat

1 jalapeño chile, stemmed, halved, seeded, and sliced thin

4 garlic cloves, minced

1 tablespoon grated fresh ginger

2 tablespoons mushroom oyster sauce or oyster sauce

1 tablespoon seasoned rice vinegar

4 scallions, sliced thin on bias, divided

why this recipe works In this easy one-skillet dinner, rich plant-based meat and creamy eggplant coexist in perfect balance amid a velvety, gingery sauce. We start by sautéing the eggplant, which releases its moisture and softens until it turns melt-in-your-mouth tender. After removing the eggplant from the pan, we sear the meat along with a jalapeño chile for a kick and some aromatic garlic and ginger just until firm crumbles form, a sign that the meat is cooked through. To finish, we simply add back the eggplant and round out the sauce with mushroom-based oyster sauce, which is plant-based (you can use traditional oyster sauce if you like), seasoned rice vinegar (which includes extra salt and sugar), and a splash of soy sauce. In just a couple minutes, the eggplant soaks up all the spicy, salty flavors in the intensely aromatic sauce. Scallions add freshness and a pop of color to this enticing weeknight meal. Serve with rice.

1 Heat 3 tablespoons oil in 12-inch nonstick skillet over medium-high heat until just smoking. Add eggplant and cook, stirring frequently, until tender and browned, about 10 minutes. Stir in 1 tablespoon soy sauce and transfer to plate.

2 Heat remaining 1 tablespoon oil in now-empty skillet over medium-high heat until shimmering. Add ground meat, jalapeño, garlic, and ginger and cook, breaking up meat with wooden spoon, until firm crumbles form, about 3 minutes.

3 Stir in oyster sauce, vinegar, and remaining 1 tablespoon soy sauce. Return eggplant and any accumulated juices to skillet and cook until warmed through, about 2 minutes. Stir in half of scallions. Serve, sprinkling with remaining scallions.

one-pan meatballs with coconut rice

serves 4
total time 1¼ hours

½ cup panko bread crumbs

2 tablespoons Asian chili-garlic sauce, plus extra for serving

2 tablespoons soy sauce, divided

1 tablespoon grated fresh ginger

12 ounces plant-based ground meat

6 scallions, sliced thin, divided

½ cup chopped fresh cilantro, divided

1 tablespoon vegetable oil

2 red bell peppers, stemmed, seeded, and sliced ¼ inch thick

1 cup long-grain white rice, rinsed

1½ cups water

⅔ cup canned coconut milk

½ teaspoon table salt

½ cup frozen peas, thawed

¼ cup dry-roasted peanuts, chopped coarse

Lime wedges

why this recipe works Boldly flavored plant-based meatballs cook up juicy and tender nestled in a skillet of creamy coconut rice in this skillet meal. The meatballs benefit from plentiful seasonings: cilantro, scallions, and ginger, plus doses of chili-garlic sauce and soy sauce for heat and savory depth. Panko bread crumbs bind the mixture and keep the meatballs moist. Chilling the meatballs helps them stay round as they brown, as does turning them frequently. After browning the meatballs, we remove them from the skillet and soften bell peppers and toast the rice. To simmer the rice, we swap out some of the water for coconut milk—just enough to provide coconutty richness without making the finished dish heavy. We return the meatballs to the skillet to finish cooking with the rice, add a handful of frozen peas off the heat to warm through, and then finish the dish with fresh cilantro and scallions, a squeeze of lime juice, and crunchy chopped peanuts. Any long-grain white rice can be substituted for the jasmine rice. You will need a 12-inch nonstick skillet with a tight-fitting lid.

1 Stir panko, chili-garlic sauce, 1 tablespoon soy sauce, and ginger in large bowl until evenly combined. Break ground meat into small pieces and add to bowl with panko mixture along with two-thirds of scallions and ¼ cup cilantro. Gently knead with your hands until mixture is well combined. Using your moistened hands, pinch off and roll meat mixture into 1½-inch meatballs. (You should have 12 meatballs.) Transfer meatballs to plate and refrigerate for at least 15 minutes or up to 24 hours.

2 Heat oil in 12-inch nonstick skillet over medium-high heat until shimmering. Add meatballs and cook until well browned all over, 2 to 3 minutes. Transfer meatballs to clean plate. Add bell peppers to fat left in skillet and cook until beginning to brown, about 3 minutes. Add rice and cook, stirring frequently, until edges of rice begin to turn translucent, about 1 minute. Stir in water, coconut milk, salt, and remaining 1 tablespoon soy sauce and bring to boil. Nestle meatballs into rice, cover skillet, reduce heat to low, and cook for 20 minutes.

3 Without removing lid, remove skillet from heat and let sit, covered, for 10 minutes. Gently stir peas into rice, then sprinkle with peanuts, remaining one-third scallions, and remaining ¼ cup cilantro. Serve with lime wedges and extra chili-garlic sauce.

spiced meat and vegetable couscous

serves 4 to 6
total time 45 minutes

¼ cup extra-virgin olive oil, divided, plus extra for drizzling

1½ cups couscous

1 zucchini, cut into ½-inch pieces

2 red bell peppers, stemmed, seeded, and cut into ½-inch pieces

½ teaspoon table salt

4 garlic cloves, minced

2 teaspoons ras el hanout

1 teaspoon grated lemon zest, plus lemon wedges for serving

12 ounces plant-based ground meat

1¾ cups vegetable broth

1 tablespoon minced fresh marjoram

why this recipe works Inspired by the alluring flavor combo of ras el hanout (a warm spice blend that usually includes cumin, cinnamon, coriander, and cloves) and lemon that's so common in many North African cuisines, we hit upon the idea of this easy, one-pan spiced couscous. We start by toasting the couscous, which gives the tiny rolled pasta an irresistible nuttiness. We then quickly sauté a colorful combination of zucchini and red bell pepper with garlic, lemon zest, and ras el hanout. Instead of browning the plant-based meat, we simply break it into pieces and add it to the skillet along with plenty of vegetable broth; this essentially braises the meat gently, so it stays ultratender. The broth hydrates the couscous and also helps flavor the meat, seamlessly marrying the two elements. We save the sprinkle of fresh marjoram until the very end so its citrusy notes come through clearly. Be aware that ras el hanout can vary in spiciness by brand. You will need a 12-inch nonstick skillet with a tight-fitting lid.

1 Heat 2 tablespoons oil in 12-inch nonstick skillet over medium-high heat until shimmering. Add couscous and cook, stirring frequently, until grains begin to brown, 3 to 5 minutes. Transfer to bowl and wipe skillet clean with paper towels.

2 Heat remaining 2 tablespoons oil in now-empty skillet over medium-high heat until just smoking. Add zucchini, bell peppers, and salt and cook until tender and lightly browned, 6 to 8 minutes. Stir in garlic, ras el hanout, and lemon zest and cook until fragrant, about 30 seconds.

3 Add ground meat, breaking up meat with wooden spoon so that pieces are no smaller than ¼ to ½ inch, then stir in broth and bring to gentle simmer. Reduce heat to medium-low, cover, and cook until firm crumbles form, about 5 minutes.

4 Remove skillet from heat and stir in couscous. Cover and let sit until liquid is absorbed and couscous is tender, about 7 minutes. Add marjoram and fluff with fork to combine. Season with salt and pepper to taste. Drizzle with extra oil and serve with lemon wedges.

keftedes and zucchini with herb-yogurt sauce

serves 4
total time 50 minutes

5   tablespoons minced fresh mint, dill, and/or parsley, divided

3   garlic cloves, minced, divided

1   teaspoon ground cumin

½   teaspoon table salt, divided

⅛   teaspoon pepper

⅛   teaspoon ground cinnamon

12 ounces plant-based ground meat

½   cup plain plant-based or dairy yogurt

1   tablespoon minced fresh chives

½   teaspoon grated lemon zest plus 1 tablespoon juice

1   tablespoon extra-virgin olive oil

1½ pounds zucchini, halved lengthwise and cut on bias into 2- to 3-inch lengths

why this recipe works Keftedes, herby Greek meatballs traditionally made with lamb, are often served as part of a meze platter with tzatziki. Here, we make them a light main by pairing them with seared zucchini and an herbed yogurt sauce. First we mix plant-based meat with mint, garlic, cumin, cinnamon, salt, and pepper and form the mixture into meatballs. The yogurt sauce is made lemony-bright with both zest and juice; chives add a mild oniony flavor, and more mint ties the flavors of the sauce and meatballs together. After a brief chill to help them keep their shape (frequent turning helps, too), the meatballs take just a few minutes to brown and cook through; searing the zucchini, which we cut on the bias into generous lengths, turns it tender and brown in just a few minutes more. For a more substantial meal, serve with bulgur, couscous, or rice.

1 Stir ¼ cup mint, two-thirds garlic, cumin, ¼ teaspoon salt, pepper, and cinnamon in large bowl until evenly combined. Break ground meat into small pieces and add to bowl with mint mixture. Gently knead with your hands until mixture is well combined. Using your moistened hands, pinch off and roll meat mixture into 1½-inch meatballs. (You should have 12 meatballs.) Transfer meatballs to plate and refrigerate for at least 15 minutes or up to 24 hours.

2 Whisk yogurt, chives, lemon zest and juice, remaining 1 tablespoon mint, and remaining garlic together in bowl and season with salt and pepper to taste. Cover and refrigerate for at least 30 minutes or up to 4 days.

3 Heat oil in 12-inch nonstick skillet over medium heat until just smoking. Add meatballs and cook, gently shaking skillet and turning meatballs frequently, until browned on all sides and meatballs register at least 135 degrees, 6 to 9 minutes. Transfer meatballs to clean plate.

4 Add zucchini cut side down to fat left in skillet and sprinkle with remaining ¼ teaspoon salt. Cook over medium-high heat, turning zucchini as needed, until tender and deep golden brown, 6 to 10 minutes. Serve meatballs with zucchini and yogurt sauce.

shepherd's pie

serves 4 to 6
total time 1¼ hours

2   pounds russet potatoes,
    peeled and cut into
    1-inch pieces

    Table salt for cooking
    potatoes

5   tablespoons extra-virgin
    olive oil, divided

1   onion, chopped fine

12 ounces plant-based
    ground meat

2   tablespoons all-purpose flour

1   tablespoon tomato paste

2   garlic cloves, minced

1   teaspoon minced
    fresh rosemary

1½ cups frozen peas and carrots

1   cup vegetable broth

¼   cup dry red wine

1   teaspoon soy sauce

¼   teaspoon pepper

why this recipe works Shepherd's pie is traditionally made with lamb (hence the "shepherd") in its United Kingdom homeland, but here in the States it's often made with beef. Either way, it's not an obvious choice for a vegetarian dinner—until plant-based meat enters the equation. With this as the base of the filling, the rest of the pie comes together quickly. Frozen peas and carrots require zero prep, and the potatoes for the fluffy topping cook while the filling comes together. To bolster the umami dimension of the savory gravy surrounding the meat and vegetables, we add tomato paste, which also promotes the formation of fond on the bottom of the pan. After topping with the mashed potatoes, we drag a fork over the topping to make ridges that brown in the oven and look fantastic. Using a frozen pea and carrot mix cuts down on prep time, but you can use fresh carrots if you prefer: Peel and chop two carrots and use 1 cup frozen peas.

1 Combine potatoes and 1 teaspoon salt in medium saucepan and cover with water by 1 inch. Bring to boil over medium-high heat and simmer until very tender, 10 to 12 minutes. Reserve 2 tablespoons cooking water, then drain potatoes and return to saucepan. Add ¼ cup oil and reserved cooking water and, using potato masher, mash until smooth. Season with salt and pepper to taste. Cover and set aside.

2 Meanwhile, heat remaining 1 tablespoon oil in 10-inch skillet over medium heat until shimmering. Add onion and cook until softened, about 5 minutes. Add ground meat and cook, breaking up meat with wooden spoon, until firm crumbles form, about 3 minutes.

3 Stir in flour, tomato paste, garlic, and rosemary and cook until fragrant, about 1 minute. Stir in peas and carrots, broth, wine, soy sauce, and pepper. Scrape up browned bits on bottom of skillet using metal spatula or wooden spoon. Bring to simmer and cook, stirring occasionally, until mixture has thickened, 3 to 5 minutes. Off heat, season with salt and pepper to taste.

4 Adjust oven rack 5 inches from broiler element and heat broiler. Using spoon, dollop potato mixture evenly over filling in skillet and smooth into even layer. Pressing gently, drag tines of fork across surface of potato mixture to make ridges. Transfer skillet to oven and broil until topping is golden brown, 6 to 8 minutes. Let cool for 10 minutes. Serve.

tamale pie

serves 6 to 8

total time 2 hours

2 tablespoons vegetable oil, divided

1 onion, chopped fine

2 (28-ounce) cans diced tomatoes, drained with 1 cup juice reserved

4 garlic cloves, minced

1¼ teaspoons table salt, divided

4 teaspoons lime juice

1 tablespoon minced canned chipotle chile in adobo sauce

12 ounces ground plant-based meat

1 tablespoon chili powder

1 teaspoon dried oregano

2 (15-ounce) cans black or pinto beans, rinsed

1½ cups fresh or thawed frozen corn

¼ cup minced fresh cilantro

4 cups water

1½ cups coarse-ground cornmeal

why this recipe works Tamales are a beloved, celebratory food in Mexico, but tamale pie is pure Tex-Mex. Featuring a lightly seasoned, tomatoey meat filling and a crisp, sweet cornbread topping, this version serves a small crowd, perfect for a laid-back Sunday supper. Canned beans and frozen corn bulk up the plant-based meat filling without adding prep work (fresh corn will also work). An onion brings sweet depth, and diced tomatoes plus a measured amount of their juice make for a saucy filling that won't bubble over and flood your oven (though baking the casserole atop a rimmed baking sheet is good insurance against any stray drips). For the topping, we mix up an easy cornmeal batter and spread it evenly over the filling. One nearly hands-off hour in the oven later and this pie is ready to be shared around the table family-style.

1 Adjust oven rack to middle position and heat oven to 375 degrees. Heat 1 tablespoon oil in 12-inch nonstick skillet until shimmering. Add onion and cook until softened, about 5 minutes. Stir in tomatoes and reserved juice, garlic, and ½ teaspoon salt and simmer until sauce is thickened, about 7 minutes. Transfer to large bowl, stir in lime juice and chipotle, and season with salt and pepper to taste; set aside. Wipe skillet clean with paper towels.

2 Heat remaining 1 tablespoon oil in now-empty skillet over medium heat until shimmering. Add ground meat and cook, breaking up meat with wooden spoon, until firm crumbles form, about 3 minutes. Add chili powder and oregano and cook until fragrant, about 30 seconds. Stir meat, beans, corn, and cilantro into tomato mixture in bowl, then transfer to 13 by 9-inch baking dish; set aside.

3 Bring water to boil in large saucepan over high heat. Add remaining ¾ teaspoon salt, then slowly pour in cornmeal, whisking vigorously to prevent lumps. Reduce heat to medium-high and cook, whisking constantly, until cornmeal begins to soften and mixture thickens, about 3 minutes. Off heat, season with salt and pepper to taste. Dollop warm cornmeal mixture evenly over casserole, then spread into even layer with rubber spatula, covering filling entirely and spreading to edges of dish.

4 Cover dish with aluminum foil, place on foil-lined rimmed baking sheet, and bake for 30 minutes. Remove foil and continue to bake until crust begins to brown and filling is bubbling at edges, 30 to 35 minutes. Let cool for 10 minutes. Serve.

skillet bratwurst with apples and brussels sprouts

serves 4
total time 35 minutes

2 tablespoons extra-virgin olive oil, divided

8 plant-based bratwurst

1½ pounds brussels sprouts, trimmed and halved or quartered if large

2 shallots, quartered

¼ teaspoon table salt

¼ teaspoon pepper

1 Gala apple, cored and cut into ½-inch wedges

1 tablespoon maple syrup or honey

1 tablespoon cider vinegar

1 tablespoon Dijon mustard

⅓ cup dried cranberries, chopped

why this recipe works It's hard to imagine a more quintessentially autumnal dinner than sausage with cabbage and apples—and it takes just a single skillet to make, to boot! When we discovered that it's possible to buy plant-based brats with all the snap and flavor of the animal-based original, we knew we had to use them in our vegan take on this dish of pure fall comfort food. We sear the brats for just a few minutes to get some browning action started, removing them from the skillet before adding brussels sprouts (essentially cute mini cabbages), quartered shallots for a light oniony note, and a sweet Gala apple cut into wedges. Once the sprouts and apple pick up some browning of their own, we flavor the mix with maple syrup, tangy cider vinegar, and Dijon mustard, and then add back the bratwurst to finish heating them through. Honeycrisp, Granny Smith, or Braeburn apples will also work in this recipe. You will need a 12-inch nonstick skillet with a tight-fitting lid.

1 Heat 1 tablespoon oil in 12-inch nonstick skillet over medium-high heat until just smoking. Add bratwurst and cook until lightly browned, about 2 minutes, turning as needed; transfer to plate and set aside.

2 Add remaining 1 tablespoon oil to now-empty skillet and heat over medium heat until shimmering. Add brussels sprouts, shallots, salt, and pepper and cook, covered, until vegetables are browned, about 5 minutes, stirring often. Stir in apple and cook until browned, about 2 minutes.

3 Whisk maple syrup, vinegar, and mustard together in bowl, then add to skillet, tossing to coat. Reduce heat to medium-low, nestle sausages into skillet, cover, and cook until brussels sprouts are tender and sausages register at least 135 degrees, 5 to 7 minutes. Sprinkle with cranberries. Serve.

sheet-pan italian sausage with peppers, onions, tomatoes, and polenta

<table>
<tr><td>serves 4</td></tr>
<tr><td>total time 40 minutes</td></tr>
</table>

12   ounces grape tomatoes

2   red bell peppers, stemmed, seeded, and sliced thin

1   onion, halved and sliced thin

3   tablespoons extra-virgin olive oil

1   garlic clove, minced

1   teaspoon minced fresh rosemary

½   teaspoon table salt

¼   teaspoon pepper

1   (18-ounce) tube cooked polenta, sliced in half lengthwise

8   plant-based Italian sausages

2   tablespoons chopped fresh basil

Plant-based or dairy Parmesan cheese (optional)

why this recipe works Two things—a rimmed baking sheet and 40 minutes of your time—are all you need to whip up a dinner that will satisfy the whole family. By coming up with a clever arrangement for all the elements and staggering their cooking times, we're able to make this three-part feast of sausage, vegetables, and polenta a weeknight reality. The juicy grape tomatoes, sweet red bell peppers, and onion take longer to cook than the plant-based sausages, so they get a head start in the oven. We also halve a log of precooked polenta and place it on the sheet pan opposite the veg to get some attractive browning. The garlic and fresh rosemary in the vegetables echo the flavors of the Italian sausage links that are the cornerstone of the meal. We arrange the sausages atop the softened vegetables and then fire up the broiler—a few minutes of the intense heat browns the sausages and caramelizes the softened vegetables. You can use store-bought Parmesan or make our Plant-Based Parmesan (page 12), if desired.

1 Adjust oven rack to upper-middle position and heat oven to 450 degrees. Spray rimmed baking sheet with vegetable oil spray. Toss tomatoes, bell peppers, onion, oil, garlic, rosemary, salt, and pepper together in large bowl. Scatter tomato mixture evenly over half of prepared sheet. Place polenta halves cut side up on empty side of prepared sheet. Roast until vegetables are softened and beginning to brown, 20 minutes.

2 Remove sheet from oven and heat broiler. Arrange sausages in single layer on top of vegetables and broil until vegetables and polenta are browned and sausages register at least 135 degrees, 5 to 8 minutes. Sprinkle with basil. Slice polenta and serve with sausages, tomato mixture, and Parmesan, if using.

stuffed zucchini with spiced meat and dried apricots

serves 4

total time 1¼ hours

4 zucchini (8 ounces each), halved lengthwise and seeded

2 tablespoons plus 1 teaspoon extra-virgin olive oil, divided

¾ teaspoon table salt, divided

½ teaspoon pepper, divided

1 onion, chopped fine

4 garlic cloves, minced

2 teaspoons ras el hanout

⅔ cup vegetable broth

½ cup medium-grind bulgur, rinsed

¼ cup dried apricots, chopped fine

8 ounces plant-based ground meat

2 tablespoons pine nuts, toasted

2 tablespoons minced fresh parsley

why this recipe works One of our favorite ways to use up a big summertime haul of zucchini is to stuff them with a hearty filling and enjoy them as the centerpiece of dinner. We particularly love the Moroccan-inspired flavors of this version made with plant-based meat, hearty bulgur, sweet dried apricots, buttery pine nuts, and ras el hanout, a warm North African spice blend. While roasting the zucchini halves to soften them, we assemble the filling. We fill the zucchini halves and then pop them back into the oven to finish, letting the oven's heat bring the fast-cooking plant-based meat to ideal doneness. Use smaller, in-season zucchini, which have thinner skins and fewer seeds. When shopping, do not confuse bulgur with cracked wheat, which has a much longer cooking time and will not work in this recipe.

1 Adjust oven racks to upper-middle and lowest positions, place rimmed baking sheet on lower rack, and heat oven to 400 degrees.

2 Brush cut sides of zucchini with 2 tablespoons oil and sprinkle with ¼ teaspoon salt and ⅛ teaspoon pepper. Lay zucchini cut side down on hot sheet and roast on lower rack until slightly softened and skins are wrinkled, 8 to 10 minutes. Remove zucchini from oven and flip cut side up; set zucchini aside, still on sheet.

3 While zucchini roast, heat remaining 1 teaspoon oil in large saucepan over medium heat until shimmering. Add onion, ¼ teaspoon salt, and ¼ teaspoon pepper and cook until softened, about 5 minutes. Stir in garlic and ras el hanout and cook until fragrant, about 30 seconds. Stir in broth, bulgur, and apricots and bring to simmer. Reduce heat to low, cover, and simmer gently until bulgur is tender, 16 to 18 minutes. Off heat, lay clean dish towel underneath lid and let sit for 10 minutes. Fluff with fork. Break ground meat into small pieces and add to bulgur mixture along with pine nuts, parsley, remaining ¼ teaspoon salt, and remaining ⅛ teaspoon pepper; mix until well combined.

4 Divide bulgur mixture evenly among each zucchini half, packing and mounding excess as needed. Bake on upper rack until filling is firm and lightly browned, 15 to 20 minutes. Serve.

stuffed eggplant with bulgur

serves 4
total time 1¾ hours

4 (10-ounce) Italian eggplants, halved lengthwise

2 tablespoons extra-virgin olive oil, divided

1¼ teaspoons table salt, divided

½ teaspoon pepper, divided

½ cup medium-grind bulgur, rinsed

¼ cup water

1 onion, chopped fine

3 garlic cloves, minced

2 teaspoons minced fresh oregano or ½ teaspoon dried

¼ teaspoon ground cinnamon

Pinch cayenne pepper

12 ounces plant-based ground meat

12 ounces plum tomatoes, cored, seeded, and chopped

2 tablespoons pine nuts, toasted

2 teaspoons red wine vinegar

2 tablespoons minced fresh parsley

why this recipe works There are countless variations on stuffed eggplant, probably because the combination of creamy, yielding eggplant with a hearty spiced filling is so undeniably good. Here we go for an Italian flavor profile and add plant-based meat to give each serving more staying power. Small Italian eggplants yield the ideal amount of food for an individual serving; we halve, cross-hatch, and roast them to eliminate excess moisture. While the eggplants roast, we mix up the filling of spiced bulgur, tomatoes, pine nuts, and meat. (As in our stuffed zucchini recipe on page 165, the meat requires no precooking since it will cook through entirely in the oven.) A sprinkle of parsley adds freshness. When shopping, do not confuse bulgur with cracked wheat, which has a much longer cooking time and will not work in this recipe.

1 Adjust oven racks to upper-middle and lowest positions, place parchment paper–lined rimmed baking sheet on lower rack, and heat oven to 400 degrees.

2 Score flesh of each eggplant half in 1-inch diamond pattern, about 1 inch deep. Brush scored sides of eggplants with 1 tablespoon oil and sprinkle with ½ teaspoon salt and ¼ teaspoon pepper. Lay eggplants cut side down on hot sheet and roast until flesh is tender, 40 to 50 minutes. Transfer eggplants cut side down to paper towel–lined baking sheet and let drain.

3 While eggplants roast, toss bulgur with water in large bowl and let sit until grains are softened and liquid is fully absorbed, 20 to 40 minutes.

4 Heat remaining 1 tablespoon oil in 12-inch nonstick skillet over medium heat until shimmering. Add onion and cook until softened, about 5 minutes. Stir in garlic, oregano, cinnamon, cayenne, and remaining ¾ teaspoon salt, and cook until fragrant, about 30 seconds. Transfer to bowl with bulgur. Break ground meat into small pieces and add to bulgur mixture along with tomatoes, pine nuts, vinegar, and remaining ¼ teaspoon pepper; mix until well combined.

5 Return eggplants cut side up to parchment-lined sheet. Using 2 forks, gently push eggplant flesh to sides to make room for filling. Divide bulgur mixture evenly among eggplant halves, packing and mounding excess as needed. Bake on upper rack until filling is firm and lightly browned, 15 to 20 minutes. Sprinkle with parsley and serve warm or at room temperature.

sheet-pan pizza with sausage, mushrooms, and cashew ricotta

serves 4 to 6
total time 1¼ hours

6 tablespoons extra-virgin olive oil, divided, plus extra for drizzling

2 pounds pizza dough, room temperature

⅔ cup (3 ounces) plant-based or dairy ricotta

2½ teaspoons grated lemon zest, divided, plus ¾ teaspoon juice

¾ teaspoon table salt, divided

12 ounces shiitake mushrooms, stemmed and sliced thin

2 tablespoons soy sauce

4 garlic cloves, minced, divided

8 ounces plant-based ground meat

2 teaspoons Sweet Italian Sausage Seasoning (page 11)

¼ cup chopped fresh parsley

Flake sea salt

why this recipe works This knockout pizza comes to the table bestrewn with mushrooms and sausagey plant-based meat, dotted with cooling dollops of ricotta (of either the plant-based or the dairy variety), and sprinkled with a refreshing parsley gremolata and crystalline flake sea salt. Using store-bought pizza dough and baking the pizza on a rimmed baking sheet takes homemade pizza from intimidating to foolproof. We fortify the earthy shiitake mushrooms with glutamate-rich soy sauce, microwaving them until softened and infused with flavor. A couple teaspoons of our homemade Italian sausage seasoning transforms the plant-based meat. Olive oil, lemon, and salt give the creamy ricotta a lift and subtle tang to balance all the rich and meaty toppings. You can use store-bought ricotta or make our Cashew Ricotta (page 12), if desired.

1 Adjust oven rack to lower-middle position and heat oven to 450 degrees. Coat rimmed baking sheet with ¼ cup oil. Press and roll dough into 16 by 12-inch rectangle on lightly floured counter. (If dough springs back during rolling, let rest for 10 minutes before rolling again.) Transfer dough to prepared sheet and stretch dough to cover sheet, pressing dough into corners. Brush top of dough with 1 tablespoon oil, cover with plastic wrap, and let rest for 20 minutes.

2 While dough rests, combine ricotta, ½ teaspoon lemon zest, lemon juice, ⅛ teaspoon salt, and remaining 1 tablespoon oil in bowl. Add water, 1 tablespoon at a time, until mixture has consistency of Greek yogurt; refrigerate until ready to use.

3 Microwave mushrooms, soy sauce, three-quarters garlic, and ½ teaspoon salt in covered bowl, stirring occasionally, until mushrooms are softened and have released their liquid, 6 to 8 minutes. Drain mushrooms, then pat dry with paper towels; set aside to cool slightly.

4 Break ground meat into small pieces in large bowl. Add Italian sausage seasoning and remaining ⅛ teaspoon salt and gently knead with your hands until well combined.

5 Sprinkle dough with reserved mushrooms, leaving ¼-inch border around edge, then pinch off ½-inch pieces of meat mixture and sprinkle over top of mushrooms. Bake until meat begins to brown, about 20 minutes, rotating pizza halfway through baking.

6 Transfer sheet to wire rack and let cool for 5 minutes. Combine parsley, remaining 2 teaspoons lemon zest, and remaining garlic in bowl. Dollop ricotta mixture over pizza in small spoonfuls, then sprinkle with parsley mixture. Drizzle with extra oil and sprinkle with sea salt. Slice and serve.

sheet-pan barbecue pizza

serves 4 to 6
total time 1½ hours

1½ pounds onions, halved and sliced ¼ inch thick through root end

6½ tablespoons water, divided

6 tablespoons extra-virgin olive oil, divided

¼ teaspoon plus ⅛ teaspoon table salt, divided

Pinch baking soda

2 pounds pizza dough, room temperature

½ cup plain plant-based or dairy yogurt

2 teaspoons grated lime zest, plus lime wedges for serving

8 ounces plant-based ground meat

2 tablespoons minced fresh cilantro plus ½ cup fresh cilantro leaves

½ teaspoon dry mustard

½ teaspoon smoked paprika

½ cup barbecue sauce

why this recipe works Our love for all things barbecue flavored is deep and wide—see the Grilled Smokehouse Barbecue Burgers (page 42) for another example. Next up for transcendence through barbecue sauce: pizza. To ensure that the smoky barbecue flavors come through loud and clear, we slather half a cup of the magical condiment over the dough as a sauce, as well as incorporate dry mustard and smoked paprika into the meaty topping so that it also takes on a smoky flavor. Caramelized onions are a great pairing with the sweet sauce; our quick caramelization method first softens the onions in a covered skillet before repeatedly pressing them against the pan's sides for efficient browning. We then combine the partially caramelized onions with some baking soda, which helps them finish caramelizing in the oven atop the pizza. The lime-yogurt drizzle adds a tangy finish to this sheet-pan pie.

1 Bring onions, 6 tablespoons water, 1 tablespoon oil, and ¼ teaspoon salt to boil in 12-inch nonstick skillet over high heat. Cover and cook until water has evaporated and onions start to sizzle, about 10 minutes.

2 Uncover, reduce heat to medium-high, and use heat-resistant rubber spatula to gently press onions into sides and bottom of skillet. Cook, without stirring, for 30 seconds. Stir onions, scraping browned bits from bottom of skillet, then gently press onions into sides and bottom of skillet again. Repeat pressing, cooking, and stirring until onions are softened, well browned, and slightly sticky, 10 to 15 minutes.

3 Combine baking soda and remaining 1½ teaspoons water in bowl. Stir baking soda solution into onions and cook, stirring constantly, until solution has evaporated, about 1 minute. Transfer onions to bowl.

4 Adjust oven rack to lower-middle position and heat oven to 450 degrees. Coat rimmed baking sheet with ¼ cup oil. Press and roll dough into 16 by 12-inch rectangle on lightly floured counter. (If dough springs back during rolling, let rest for 10 minutes before rolling again.) Transfer dough to prepared sheet and stretch dough to cover sheet, pressing dough into corners. Brush top of dough with remaining 1 tablespoon oil, cover with plastic wrap, and let rest for 20 minutes.

5 While dough rests, combine yogurt and lime zest in bowl; refrigerate until ready to use. Break ground meat into small pieces in large bowl. Add minced cilantro, dry mustard, paprika, and remaining ⅛ teaspoon salt, and gently knead with your hands until well combined.

6 Spread barbecue sauce over dough, leaving ¼-inch border around edge. Sprinkle onions evenly over sauce, then pinch off ½-inch pieces of meat mixture and sprinkle over top. Bake until meat begins to brown, about 20 minutes, rotating pizza halfway through baking.

7 Transfer sheet to wire rack and let cool for 5 minutes. Drizzle with yogurt sauce and sprinkle with cilantro leaves. Slice and serve with lime wedges.

nutritional information for our recipes

To calculate the nutritional values of our recipes per serving, we used The Food Processor SQL by ESHA research. When using this program, we entered all the ingredients, using weights for important ingredients such as most vegetables. We also used our preferred brands in these analyses. We did not include additional salt or pepper for food that's "seasoned to taste." Any ingredient listed as "optional" was excluded from the analyses. For recipes with a range in the number of servings, we used the highest number in the range to calculate the nutritional values.

	calories	total fat (g)	sat fat (g)	chol (mg)	sodium (mg)	total carb (g)	dietary fiber (g)	total sugars (g)	protein (g)
plant-based basics									
Italian Meatball Seasoning (per teaspoon)	10	0	0	0	580	2	0	0	0
Breakfast Sausage Seasoning (per teaspoon)	10	0	0	0	100	3	0	2	0
Sweet Italian Sausage Seasoning (per teaspoon)	10	0	0	0	0	2	1	1	0
Hot Italian Sausage Seasoning	*5*	*0*	*0*	*0*	*0*	*1*	*1*	*0*	*0*
Mexican Chorizo Seasoning (per tablespoon)	20	0.5	0	0	50	4	2	2	1
Plant-Based Mayonnaise (per tablespoon)	180	20	3	0	75	0	0	0	0
Plant-Based Parmesan (per tablespoon)	50	3.5	0.5	0	115	3	0	0	2
Cashew Ricotta (per 2 tablespoons)	110	10	1.5	0	75	4	1	1	3
with Roasted Red Peppers	*120*	*10*	*1.5*	*0*	*120*	*5*	*1*	*2*	*3*
with Chipotle and Lime	*110*	*10*	*1.5*	*0*	*75*	*4*	*1*	*1*	*3*
with Sun-Dried Tomatoes and Rosemary	*130*	*10*	*1.5*	*0*	*95*	*6*	*1*	*1*	*3*
Plant-Based Pie Dough (per ¼ dough round)	470	32	29	0	290	42	0	3	5
snacks and apps									
Meaty Loaded Nacho Dip	120	7	1.5	0	380	11	2	1	4
Lemony Hummus with Baharat-Spiced Topping	170	12	2.5	0	340	10	3	0	7
Summer Rolls	420	5	5	0	640	49	3	5	17
Egg Rolls	220	12	3.5	0	1280	18	3	6	11
Stuffed Grape Leaves	110	5	1.5	0	230	13	1	1	5
Classic Pub Sliders	250	14	5	0	500	20	1	3	10

	calories	total fat (g)	sat fat (g)	chol (mg)	sodium (mg)	total carb (g)	dietary fiber (g)	total sugars (g)	protein (g)
snacks and apps (cont.)									
Cilantro-Lime Sliders with Pickled Cucumbers and Peanut Sauce	230	11	4	0	470	20	2	5	11
Jamaican Meat Patties	580	39	32	0	510	46	2	2	13
Albóndigas en Salsa de Almendras	160	9	3.5	0	400	9	2	1	8
Pesto Cocktail Meatballs	260	20	4.5	0	480	12	3	3	10
Pan-Fried Dumplings	190	9	2.5	5	490	17	1	1	8
burgers, sandwiches, tacos, and more									
Classic Burgers Your Way	380	18	9	0	660	31	3	3	23
Grilled Smokehouse Barbecue Burgers	430	16	7	0	1350	50	5	19	20
Baharat-Spiced Burgers with Beet Tzatziki	440	25	8	0	880	33	4	6	21
Italian Sausage Burgers with Broccoli Rabe and Red Peppers	550	37	9	0	930	35	3	7	20
Chorizo Burgers with Pineapple and Poblanos	480	28	8	0	710	40	5	9	20
Meatloaf Burgers with Crispy Smashed Tater Tots	460	23	7	0	960	45	3	11	20
Double Smashie Burgers	540	33	11	0	1160	43	3	8	20
Larb Lettuce Wraps with Lime, Mint, and Cilantro	230	11	6	0	790	16	4	4	17
Pita Sandwiches with Cucumber-Yogurt Sauce	460	19	7	0	820	48	4	4	25
Grilled Kofte Wraps	430	28	10	0	680	22	5	3	25
Meat-Lover's Veggie Banh Mi	610	33	8	0	2010	54	5	10	22
Italian Meatball Subs with Broccoli	780	41	15	0	1680	66	9	10	31
Bratwurst Sandwiches with Red Potato and Kale Salad	690	40	9	0	1630	54	2	6	25
Breakfast Sausage Sandwiches	410	25	6	0	310	30	3	5	18
with Fried Eggs	*510*	*33*	*8*	*185*	*420*	*31*	*3*	*5*	*24*
Breakfast Tacos	680	29	8	0	2170	78	5	9	28
with Scrambled Eggs	*710*	*32*	*10*	*280*	*2280*	*77*	*5*	*9*	*30*
Not-from-a-Box Weeknight Tacos	280	16	5	0	610	25	6	2	12
Crispy Fried Tacos with Almonds and Raisins	450	28	6	0	620	39	3	7	14
Chorizo and Potato Tacos with Salsa Verde	440	22	5	0	600	52	5	6	13

	calories	total fat (g)	sat fat (g)	chol (mg)	sodium (mg)	total carb (g)	dietary fiber (g)	total sugars (g)	protein (g)
burgers, sandwiches, tacos, and more (cont.)									
Chorizo, Corn, and Tomato Tostadas with Lime Crema	440	20	6	0	1060	54	5	8	15
Meat-and-Bean Burritos	680	35	9	0	1570	69	11	5	28
Empanadas with Olives and Raisins	1190	78	65	0	1200	98	3	12	26
pasta, noodles, and bowls									
Big-Batch Weeknight Meat Sauce	110	5	2	0	390	11	3	4	7
Tagliatelle with Weeknight Bolognese	470	13	4.5	0	810	65	5	4	20
Spaghetti with Sausage and Spring Vegetables	500	16	5	0	480	69	8	6	23
Orecchiette with Broccoli Rabe and Sausage	430	11	4.5	0	310	63	6	2	22
Meatballs and Marinara	510	13	4.5	0	610	75	6	7	22
Pasta with Sausage, Mushrooms, and Peas	680	19	7	0	740	90	7	11	33
Meaty Skillet Mac	500	16	7	0	1930	66	9	11	25
Toasted Orzo Pilaf with Meatballs, Fennel, and Orange	590	23	8	0	1190	66	6	7	26
One-Pot Stroganoff	590	25	9	60	1460	61	3	4	26
Dan Dan Mian	520	25	6	10	1340	54	2	4	21
Savory Soba Noodles with Eggplant and Miso	650	24	8	0	800	84	6	9	26
Lion's Head Meatballs with Cabbage and Rice Noodles	360	14	8	0	1400	33	5	4	22
Bun Cha	480	14	6	0	1230	68	5	12	21
Rice Noodle Bowl with Scallion-Meat Patties and Cucumber	520	23	8	0	1660	58	3	2	21
Meaty Zoodle Bowl with Mango and Garam Masala	370	22	7	0	590	26	4	7	19
Spinach and Snap Pea Salad Bowl with Herbed Meat Patties	420	28	8	0	840	28	9	11	19
Taco Salad Bowl	310	14	5	0	820	36	4	5	16
Lemony Brown Rice Bowl with Meatballs and Sun-Dried Tomatoes	450	18	7	0	860	57	7	1	20
Quinoa Bowl with Meatballs, Green Beans, and Garlic Dressing	660	32	9	0	910	67	9	12	26
Farro Bowl with Butternut Squash, Sausage, and Radicchio	600	28	7	0	540	75	11	20	18

	calories	total fat (g)	sat fat (g)	chol (mg)	sodium (mg)	total carb (g)	dietary fiber (g)	total sugars (g)	protein (g)
soup-pot, skillet, and sheet-pan meals									
Italian Wedding Soup	300	10	4.5	0	840	36	5	3	16
Kimchi, Meat, and Tofu Soup	260	13	4.5	0	1250	16	2	7	15
Green Chile Stew with Hominy	400	16	7	0	1500	46	11	12	19
Weeknight Meaty Chili	240	10	3.5	0	960	26	7	8	13
Black Bean, Sweet Potato, and Zucchini Chili	320	13	4	0	870	37	6	8	15
Skillet Chipotle Chili with Lime-Cilantro Crema	390	14	4.5	0	1210	51	4	6	18
Mapo Tofu	390	27	4	0	1110	15	3	2	18
Keema	200	13	4.5	0	510	10	3	3	11
Cuban Picadillo	280	13	4.5	0	680	23	3	12	11
One-Pot Rice and Lentils with Spiced Meat	510	25	10	0	980	54	6	3	19
Sautéed Eggplant with Polenta	690	40	10	0	1330	64	12	17	21
Sautéed Eggplant with Soy, Ginger, and Scallions	370	25	7	0	1020	21	7	8	18
One-Pan Meatballs with Coconut Rice	590	27	14	0	1290	63	6	4	25
Spiced Meat and Vegetable Couscous	400	17	5	0	610	44	5	2	16
Keftedes and Zucchini with Herb-Yogurt Sauce	280	17	7	0	580	15	4	5	18
Shepherd's Pie	390	19	6	0	520	41	5	2	15
Tamale Pie	340	10	3.5	0	1200	50	9	6	15
Skillet Bratwurst with Apples and Brussels Sprouts	610	32	11	0	1280	49	9	23	38
Sheet-Pan Italian Sausage with Peppers, Onions, Tomatoes, and Polenta	640	35	0	0	1580	46	3	6	36
Stuffed Zucchini with Spiced Meat and Dried Apricots	360	19	6	0	770	35	7	11	16
Stuffed Eggplant with Bulgur	440	21	7	0	1020	44	14	13	21
Sheet-Pan Pizza with Sausage, Mushrooms, and Cashew Ricotta	650	28	7	0	1640	81	3	11	22
Sheet-Pan Barbecue Pizza	690	25	6	0	1400	96	3	22	20

conversions and equivalents

Some say cooking is a science and an art. We would say that geography has a hand in it, too. Flours and sugars manufactured in the United Kingdom and elsewhere will feel and taste different from those manufactured in the United States. So we cannot promise that the loaf of bread you bake in Canada or England will taste the same as a loaf baked in the States, but we can offer guidelines for converting weights and measures. We also recommend that you rely on your instincts when making our recipes. Refer to the visual cues provided. If the dough hasn't "come together in a ball" as described, you may need to add more flour—even if the recipe doesn't tell you to. You be the judge.

The recipes in this book were developed using standard U.S. measures following U.S. government guidelines. The charts below offer equivalents for U.S. and metric measures. All conversions are approximate and have been rounded up or down to the nearest whole number.

example

1 teaspoon = 4.9292 milliliters, rounded up to 5 milliliters
1 ounce = 28.3495 grams, rounded down to 28 grams

volume conversions

u.s.	metric
1 teaspoon	5 milliliters
2 teaspoons	10 milliliters
1 tablespoon	15 milliliters
2 tablespoons	30 milliliters
¼ cup	59 milliliters
⅓ cup	79 milliliters
½ cup	118 milliliters
¾ cup	177 milliliters
1 cup	237 milliliters
1¼ cups	296 milliliters
1½ cups	355 milliliters
2 cups (1 pint)	473 milliliters
2½ cups	591 milliliters
3 cups	710 milliliters
4 cups (1 quart)	0.946 liter
1.06 quarts	1 liter
4 quarts (1 gallon)	3.8 liters

weight conversions

ounces	grams
½	14
¾	21
1	28
1½	43
2	57
2½	71
3	85
3½	99
4	113
4½	128
5	142
6	170
7	198
8	227
9	255
10	283
12	340
16 (1 pound)	454

conversions for common baking ingredients

Baking is an exacting science. Because measuring by weight is far more accurate than measuring by volume, and thus more likely to produce reliable results, in our recipes we provide ounce measures in addition to cup measures for many ingredients. Refer to the chart below to convert these measures into grams.

ingredient	ounces	grams
Flour		
1 cup all-purpose flour*	5	142
1 cup cake flour	4	113
1 cup whole-wheat flour	5½	156
Sugar		
1 cup granulated (white) sugar	7	198
1 cup packed brown sugar (light or dark)	7	198
1 cup confectioners' sugar	4	113
Cocoa Powder		
1 cup cocoa powder	3	85
Butter†		
4 tablespoons (½ stick or ¼ cup)	2	57
8 tablespoons (1 stick or ½ cup)	4	113
16 tablespoons (2 sticks or 1 cup)	8	227

* U.S. all-purpose flour, the most frequently used flour in this book, does not contain leaveners, as some European flours do. These leavened flours are called self-rising or self-raising. If you are using self-rising flour, take this into consideration before adding leaveners to a recipe.

† In the United States, butter is sold both salted and unsalted. We generally recommend unsalted butter. If you are using salted butter, take this into consideration before adding salt to a recipe.

oven temperatures

fahrenheit	celsius	gas mark
225	105	¼
250	120	½
275	135	1
300	150	2
325	165	3
350	180	4
375	190	5
400	200	6
425	220	7
450	230	8
475	245	9

converting temperatures from an instant-read thermometer

We include doneness temperatures in many of the recipes in this book. We recommend an instant-read thermometer for the job. Refer to the table above to convert Fahrenheit degrees to Celsius. Or, for temperatures not represented in the chart, use this simple formula:

Subtract 32 degrees from the Fahrenheit reading, then divide the result by 1.8 to find the Celsius reading.

example
"Cook burger patties until meat registers 130 to 135 degrees."

To convert:
$130°F – 32 = 98°$
$98° ÷ 1.8 = 54.44°C$, rounded down to 54°C

index

Note: Page references in *italics* indicate photographs.